THE $7 A MEAL MEDITERRANEAN COOKBOOK

FEED A FAMILY FOR $7 OR LESS

301 DELICIOUS, NUTRITIOUS RECIPES THE WHOLE FAMILY WILL LOVE

Dawn Altomari-Rathjen, LPN, BPS,
Jennifer M. Bendelius, MS, RD, and Leah Traverse, RD

adamsmedia
Avon, Massachusetts

Published by
Adams Media, a division of F+W Media, Inc.
57 Littlefield Street, Avon, MA 02322. U.S.A.
www.adamsmedia.com

ISBN 10: 1-4405-1142-X
ISBN 13: 978-1-4405-1142-4
eISBN 10: 1-4405-1145-4
eISBN 13: 978-1-4405-1145-5

Printed in the United States of America.

10 9 8 7 6 5 4 3 2 1

Library of Congress Cataloging-in-Publication Data
Altomari-Rathjen, Dawn.
The $7 a meal Mediterranean cookbook / Dawn Altomari-Rathjen, Jennifer M. Bendelius, and Leah Traverse.
p. cm.
Includes index.
ISBN-13: 978-1-4405-1142-4
ISBN-10: 1-4405-1142-X
ISBN-10: 978-1-44051-145-5 (ebook)
ISBN-10: 1-4405-1145-4 (ebook)
1. Cooking, Mediterranean. 2. Low budget cooking. 3. Cookbooks. I. Bendelius, Jennifer. II. Traverse, Leah. III. Title.
TX725.M35A479   2011
641.59822—dc22   2010039129

This book is available at quantity discounts for bulk purchases.
For information, please call 1-800-289-0963.

CONTENTS

INTRODUCTION

The bountiful cuisine of the Mediterranean evokes thoughts of luscious grains, pasta, vegetables, fruits, and, of course, olive oil. The colorful vegetables and rich taste of olive oil make this cuisine a feast for the eyes as well as the taste buds. The unique flavors of these regions have caused some enthusiasts to call this the best cuisine on earth!

Cooking delicious Mediterranean dishes on a budget may seem like an impossible feat, but this book has made it easy for you. By preparing simple but appetizing meals from scratch, you will automatically spend less money. Just think of all the people who have to make money in a restaurant: the owners, suppliers, cooks, wait staff, and cleaning crew. You are paying their salaries when you eat out. So of course that food is more expensive. Also, cooking at home allows you to choose what goes into your recipe. Not only will you be able to create healthier options; you also will get to decide whether to buy a fancier ingredient or stick to the budget-friendly ones. In the end, you're the one in control of your budget.

Sale prices, discounts, and coupons were not included in the price calculations in this book, so you may find that prices in your area are higher or lower than those stated here. Every cook is different, and so is every kitchen. These recipes were developed with cost savings in mind. Each recipe includes its cost per serving, and many also have a note explaining how to make the recipe more special and expensive if you want to splurge. Now get ready to whip up flavorful appetizers, entrées, sauces, and more! *Buon appetito!*

CHAPTER 1

COOKING ON A BUDGET

We used to joke that every time we turned around, prices went up. Now we know it's true! Food prices in particular are affected by many factors, including the price of oil, commodities speculation on the stock market, conversion of food to fuel, the growth in world population, and changes in the climate and weather. Studies and surveys show that most of us are abandoning restaurants and fast-food places and are trying to cook and eat at home. It's true: You can control your budget—and still eat very well, for very little—as long as you learn some new habits and follow a few simple rules.

IT'S ALL ABOUT THE PLAN

Everything should start with a plan, whether you're making a household budget, searching for a job, or trying to feed your family on less money. If you write lists, plan menus, and cut coupons, you will save a significant amount of money, and you will be able to serve your family tastier and more nutritious food.

COOK AT HOME

Here's the most important rule: You will save money if you cook at home. The more work you do, and the simpler, more basic foods you buy, the more money you will save. This may sound daunting, but once you get into the habit of cooking it will take you less and less time and the skill will become second nature. Choose to make your own meals and you will control what's in the food you feed your family.

Eating "lower on the food chain" doesn't just mean avoiding beef, pork, and chicken. It also means eating foods that are as close to harvest condition as possible. A ripe peach will be less expensive than ice cream made with peaches, or a bottled peach salsa. Manufactured foods will almost always cost more than the raw ingredients assembled by you.

WHAT'S CHEAPER?

A lot of your grocery savings will depend on what you buy. It's important to know that buying whole chicken breasts and deboning them yourself will not only cost less but give you more for your money. The bones and skin can be saved to make chicken stock. In fact, for all of the chicken recipes in this book I recommend buying bone-in, skin-on chicken breasts and removing the large breast muscle yourself. If you do this, a boneless, skinless chicken breast will cost you about a dollar. Buying them already boned and skinned will cost almost $2 apiece.

Surprisingly, butter costs about 10 cents a tablespoon, while the least expensive form of olive oil is 20 cents per tablespoon. When you're frying sesame cheese puffs, stuffed onions, or other Mediterranean foods and want the best taste, butter and olive oil are the best choices. Use butter for the best flavor, and add a bit of the more expensive olive oil to raise the smoke point and keep the butter from burning.

Frozen and canned vegetables will usually be cheaper than fresh. And don't worry about the nutrition of these products. Processed produce has just as many vitamins as fresh; in many cases, even more because it's processed within a few hours of harvest. Fresh vegetables and fruits, especially when out of season, take days to get to the market, and every day they lose vitamin content.

Buying a cheaper top round steak and marinating it overnight in the fridge will result in a tender and flavorful cut of beef that just takes a bit more work than plopping a tenderloin or rib eye on the grill. And buying that same steak and pounding it with flour makes Swiss steaks cheaper than you'll find in a frozen dinner. Make your own hamburgers rather than buying preformed patties. You get the idea!

Unit pricing is one of the best tools for budget shopping. Look at the price per ounce to see if that huge box of pasta is a better buy than the smaller one. Most grocery stores have unit pricing tags on the shelves right under the product. You can also bring a calculator to the store to figure it out for yourself. Just divide the price by the number of ounces in the product and compare.

Look at the price of a head of lettuce versus the bagged, "pre-washed" assembled salads. The price is more than double, for less product! The lesson? The more work you do in the kitchen, the more money you will save.

LOOK AT YOUR SPENDING HABITS

When you draw up a budget, it's important to look at how you have spent money in the past. We fall into habits and patterns and do what's easiest, especially when our lives are busy and stressful. By taking a close look at how you spend money on food, you can save a lot and eat better at the same time.

Look through your checkbook and credit card receipts and add up how much you've spent on food in the last two months, including restaurant meals, fast-food stops, and trips to the convenience store as well as regular grocery shopping. Break down the different categories, add everything up, and then decide where you want to cut down.

Do you eat out because you love certain dishes, like Chicken Saltimbocca or Lamb Samosas? Learn to make your favorite Mediterranean foods at home, and not only will you be saving money, but you'll learn something about the world. The cooking methods, herbs and spices, and foods from all around the Mediterranean are usually quick to make, easy, and inexpensive.

If you're like most Americans, you spend a lot of money eating out; in fact, almost 50 percent of our food budget is spent on food not prepared at home. While it's fun to eat out, you can prepare the same meal at home for less than half the cost. Italian, Greek, Spanish, and even Middle Eastern cuisine and recipes can easily be made in your own kitchen for a fraction of restaurant food. It's just as authentic, you don't have to worry about food safety or the nutrition of the food, and you can make cooking and baking a family event.

THE INDISPENSABLE LIST

All right, let's get serious. To start cooking on a budget, first you need to know what you have in the house, what your family likes to eat, and what you know you can cook. Then you have to make a list every time you go grocery shopping. And stick to it!

RECORD THE EVIDENCE

To get started, go through your pantry, fridge, and freezer and take stock. For two weeks, make a list of the staples your family uses. For instance, every week you may buy milk, bread, cereal, ground beef, carrots, tomatoes, and rice. Use these foods to create a master list to save time. Then post that master list on the refrigerator, and when you run out of a food make a note on the list.

The rest of your list should come from ingredients you need for your planned meals. Note the amounts you'll need and any specifics on the list. When you go shopping, abide by the list. But at the same time,

be open to change! You may find that there are in-store specials on certain foods, especially meats, which may change your meal plan. Be flexible and look for good buys.

EASY LIST-MAKING

Websites can be a valuable source of information. Many sites, like *www.web momz.com* and *www.ehow.com*, offer printable grocery list forms already divided into categories that you just fill in. And you can personalize the list too, adding your staple items that you buy every week.

For some fun browsing on the web, as well as ideas for shopping lists, take a look at *www.grocery lists.org*, which is a collection of grocery lists found abandoned on supermarket floors and in parking lots. It's fun to see what other people buy, and you can learn something, too!

In some cases, you may want to include quantity on your list, especially for more expensive items like spices or seafood. For instance, you can buy small amounts of spices and nuts in bulk bins at most food co-ops. Unless you know that you will use a particular food again, this is the cheapest way to shop.

Now follow the list. It should be your guide when you're in the store. Concentrating on it will help keep you focused on the foods you need and will help distract your attention from foods that look and smell tempting but that aren't in your budget. You'll also discover that shopping this way will take less time and be less stressful.

USING COUPONS

You've seen those news stories about women who buy a full cart of groceries for $2.18. While doing so is possible, saving that much money on groceries with coupons is practically a full-time job and requires double-couponing as well as buying many prepackaged and processed foods. By using the following tips and shopping wisely, you can use coupons to cut 10–20 percent from your grocery bill.

When you are looking for a coupon, think about these things:

- Will the coupon make that item the cheapest in unit pricing?
- Will you be able to use all of the food before the expiration date?
- Does your family like this food, and will they eat it?
- Is the food nutritious or junk food?
- Can you easily use the food in your regular in meal planning?
- Request coupons from manufacturers by calling the 800 numbers on their products.

Spend a little money and buy a loose-leaf notebook, along with a file folder to hold menus and coupons. You can arrange the folder in several ways: according to the types of food, according to the layout of your grocery store, or according to expiration date. Be sure you understand what food the coupon applies to, and buy that exact product. And go through the folder often, making a note of which coupons you want to use and which ones are close to their expiration date.

Sign up for coupon sites on the Internet that offer free, printable coupons, like *Cool Savings.com*, *SmartSource.com*, *RetailMeNot .com/Coupons/Food*, and *TheGroceryGame .com*. Then each week you'll be reminded via e-mail to check those sites for new coupons. Be sure to only use coupons for foods you know your family likes. And look for "free" coupons, which will let you try a product before you spend money on it.

Make sure to read the fine print on the coupons carefully. Sometimes you can use more than one coupon on a product, and if that product happens to be on sale, the savings can really add up. More often, you need to purchase the size and brand of product that matches the coupon exactly.

If a store runs out of an item you have a coupon for, or that is on sale, ask for a rain check, and then keep that rain check in the coupon folder. When the item is restocked, the grocery store will mail you a notice, and you can buy it at the sale price.

GROCERY SHOPPING

The layout of grocery stores is planned to keep you in the store for a long period of time and to encourage you to spend the most money possible. After all, the grocer needs to make a profit! But when you know the tricks that are used, you can learn to avoid them and save money while still feeding your family well.

KNOW THE STORE

Many stores offer "reward plans" that can help you save money. Some stores offer discounts on gasoline tied to the amount of food you buy. Others have punch cards that you can redeem for special products or money off when the card is full. Learn about these programs and use as many as you possibly can.

Learn the layout of the stores you patronize most often, so you can get in and out as quickly as possible and so you don't waste time looking for products. If you can't find a product fairly quickly, ask! Any store employee will be able to tell you where something is located.

You can also get help at the butcher counter. You can always ask if the butcher will cut a larger roast or steak into a smaller portion for you at the same price as the full cut. Ask if she'll divide up a package of chicken drumsticks or wings. She's also a great source of information if you have questions about how to prepare a certain cut of meat.

And when you're looking for something, avoid products placed at eye level. That's the "premium space" that brand-name producers want, and where the highest-priced products are located. Also avoid "end caps," those displays at the end of the aisle. Products that are placed there appear to be on sale, when more often they are not.

CHECK YOUR RECEIPT

Even with digital machines and scanners, there will be mistakes on your receipt. Check to make sure that the correct prices, especially sale prices, are on your receipt, that the coupons you turn in are properly redeemed for the correct price, and that there weren't any products that were scanned twice.

If you do find a mistake, don't go back to the cashier. Go directly to the service counter and speak to someone there. That way you'll get your money back, you won't hold up a line, and the correct price or discount will be programmed into all the checkout computers.

SHOP ONCE A WEEK

Most budget books tell you to shop only once a week. If you are organized and know that you'll use the food you buy within that time, this is a smart idea, not only for your food budget, but your gasoline budget as well.

But if you let food go to waste, if you throw a frozen pizza into the oven instead of slicing the vegetables and making that quiche you had planned, it's better to shop more often and buy less at one time. This works best if a grocery store with good prices is on your route home from work or school. Combine errands to save on gas, but make sure to shop for groceries last. Perishable and frozen foods should go directly from the grocery store to your fridge and freezer, as quickly as possible.

The number of times you shop in a week also depends on how far you are from a grocery store. If there is one with reasonable prices and good stock within walking distance, you can shop more often, look for buys, and take advantage of coupons and sales.

WASTE: THE BUDGET BUSTER

The biggest budget buster isn't that $8 steak or $4 gallon of milk. It's waste!

Americans throw away as much as 45 percent of the food they buy. If you spend $800 a month on food, you may be throwing away more than $300 a month. Whether it's a head of lettuce that languishes in the fridge until it wilts, or a bag of chicken breasts imperfectly wrapped so it develops freezer burn, food is easy to waste.

HOW LONG DO FOODS LAST?

How long should perishable products be kept on the counter or in the fridge until they're no longer safe or wholesome? There are some fairly rigid rules about how soon food should be used before it must be frozen or thrown away. For manufactured and dairy products, and some meat products, be sure to scrupulously follow the expiration dates stamped on the package. For others, here are some general rules.

SHELF LIFE

FOOD	ON COUNTER	REFRIGERATOR	FREEZER
Apples	3 days	3 weeks	Cook first, 6 months
Strawberries	1 day	3 days	Flash freeze, 4 months
Berries	1 day	2 days	4 months
Onions	3 weeks	Not recommended	Cooked, 6 months
Potatoes	1 month	Not recommended	Cooked, 6 months
Mushrooms	1 day	3 days	8 months
Celery	1 day	1 week	Not recommended
Ground meat	Not recommended	3 days	6 months
Eggs	Not recommended	3 weeks	Separated, 3 months
Cheese	Not recommended	3 weeks	6 months

Leftovers have to be planned into your budget to make another meal. Spend a little money to get reusable good-quality food containers that will hold the food until you're ready to use it. Always refrigerate food promptly, know what's in your fridge and freezer, and plan your weekly meals with leftovers in mind.

FOOD SAVERS

There are some products you can buy that can help reduce waste. Green Bags made by Evert-Fresh do work, although some sources say the food doesn't stay fresh as long as claimed. The bag should keep your strawberries and asparagus fresh and wholesome for 5–7 days, which is 3–4 days longer than produce will stay fresh without them.

You can also look into vacuum sealers, which remove the air from food containers to help prevent freezer burn. Of course, you can get close to the same result this way: Use a heavy-duty freezer bag, seal it almost to the end, then insert a straw and suck out as much air as possible. Seal the bag, label, and freeze it immediately

BUY IN BULK

Bulk buying has long been the secret of organizations, schools, and restaurants. Food is almost always cheaper bought in large quantities. However, you don't have to lug home gallon-size cans of peaches or a dozen loaves of bread to take advantage of bulk buying.

If you have storage space, and are willing to scrupulously follow expiration dates and rotate the food, you can save lots of money buying in bulk, especially from bulk bins at co-ops. Bring your own containers, and be sure to mark everything on masking tape placed on the container: date of purchase, the name of the item, quantity, and expiration dates, if any.

Be sure to follow cleanliness instructions when buying in bulk. Put on gloves when you remove food from a bulk bin, and use the tongs or scoops supplied. Ask about expiration dates and times for food. And be sure to place food in tightly sealed, clean containers and store it in a cool, dark place.

You could also share costs with another family if you want to buy in bulk. Pair up with another family or two and buy mayonnaise, canned fruit, milk, cereal, and meat in large quantities, then divide them equally.

LEARN TO COOK

Cooking isn't difficult; it just takes some time to become familiar with new terms and some practice sessions to learn some skills. Watch cooking shows on television; that's one of the best ways to learn how to cook and bake.

You can find lots of places that offer cooking e-courses and information online free of charge. Go to the library and take out a basic cookbook and read through it. You can always ask questions on online forums. Your local Extension Service, administered through the land-grant university in your area, is also a good resource for cooking information, as well as recipes and food safety tips.

Here are some basic rules for cooking and baking:

- First, read through the recipe.
- If you don't understand words or terms, look them up.
- Make sure you have the ingredients and utensils on hand.
- Follow the directions carefully.
- Be sure you understand how to measure ingredients.
- Measure flour by lightly spooning it into the measuring cup, then level off the top.
- Start checking the food at the shortest cooking time.
- Understand doneness tests.
- Make sure meat is cooked to a safe internal temperature.

Some supermarkets and specialty stores also occasionally offer cooking classes. Take the time to ask neighbors, family, and friends about teaching you to cook. Once you've learned the basic rules about cooking and baking, you'll be able to save money in many ways.

It may feel a little awkward and strange during your first forays into the kitchen, but as with any skill, the more you practice, the easier it will become. And when you see that your budget is balancing and you're saving money, you'll be encouraged to stick with it. There are more advantages to cooking for yourself, too; you'll spend more time with family, enjoy the family table, and teach your kids how to cook and feed themselves, which will set them up for life.

Now let's get started in the kitchen with these delicious and easy recipes that cost less than $7 to prepare, and feed at least four people.

CHAPTER 2

BREAKFAST

Breakfast Bruschetta

 Serves 4

Total Cost: $5.71

Calories per Serving: 556

Fat: 41.6 grams

Protein: 13.1 grams

Sodium: 461.9 mg

Carbohydrates: 33.3 grams

Cholesterol: 10.8 mg

½ loaf Italian or French bread

½ cup extra-virgin olive oil

¼ cup pesto (see recipes in Chapter 5)

1 medium tomato

2 egg whites

2 whole eggs

1 roasted red pepper (for roasting instructions see Bruschetta with Marinated Red Pepper recipe in Chapter 3)

¼ cup mozzarella cheese

1. Slice the bread into 4¾-inch lengthwise pieces. Brush one side of each with a bit of the oil; toast on grill. When that side is toasted, brush oil on the other side, flip, and toast that side.
2. Place the toasted bread on a sheet pan and spread with pesto. Peel and chop the tomato; combine it with the egg whites and whole eggs. Dice the pepper and shred the cheese.
3. Heat the remaining oil in a sauté pan to medium temperature; add the egg mixture and cook omelet style. Cut the omelet and place on the bread; top with cheese and red pepper.

Roasted Potatoes with Vegetables

 Serves 6

$ Total Cost: $3.12

Calories per Serving: 156

Fat: 4.7 grams

Protein: 3.5 grams

Sodium: 82 mg

Carbohydrates: 26.5 grams

Cholesterol: 0 mg

3 Idaho baking potatoes

1 sweet potato

3 carrots

1 yellow onion

½ pound button mushrooms

2 tablespoons olive oil

Kosher salt, to taste

Fresh-cracked black pepper, to taste

1. Preheat oven to 400°F.
2. Large-dice the potatoes and carrots. Large-dice the onion. Trim off any discolored ends from the mushroom stems.
3. In a large bowl, mix together the olive oil, potatoes, carrots, onions, and mushrooms. Place them evenly in a roasting pan, and sprinkle with salt and pepper.
4. Roast the vegetables for 30 to 45 minutes, until tender. Serve warm.

The $7 a Meal Mediterranean Cookbook

Frittata

 Serves 6

1 pound Idaho potatoes

2 each yellow and red peppers

2 Italian green peppers

1 large red onion

½ cup fresh oregano

3 ounces fontina cheese

2 teaspoons olive oil

Kosher or sea salt, to taste

Fresh-cracked black pepper, to taste

3 whole eggs

6 egg whites

1 cup plain nonfat yogurt

1 cup skim milk

1. Preheat oven to 375°F.
2. Slice the potatoes into large pieces. Stem, seed, and slice the peppers. Cut the onion into thick slices. Chop the oregano leaves. Grate the fontina.
3. Separately toss the potatoes, peppers, and onion in oil, and drain on a rack. Season with salt and black pepper.
4. Roast all the vegetables separately in the oven until partially cooked. Layer all in a baking dish.
5. Whisk together the eggs, egg whites, yogurt, milk, and grated cheese; pour into the baking dish. Bake until the egg mixture is completely set, approximately 30 to 45 minutes. Sprinkle with chopped oregano and serve.

For the Meat Lover
Generally speaking, Americans are meat eaters. If you are one of the many who think a breakfast just isn't a breakfast without some type of pork product, then consider adding chopped bacon, sausage, or ham to this recipe.

Rye-Pumpernickel Strata with Bleu Cheese

 Serves 6

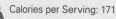

Total Cost: $2.24

Calories per Serving: 171

Fat: 6 grams

Protein: 11.7 grams

Sodium: 445.7 mg

Carbohydrates: 17.5 grams

Cholesterol: 80.4 mg

3 (1½-inch) slices seedless rye bread

3 (1½-inch) slices pumpernickel bread

½ teaspoon extra-virgin olive oil

2 whole eggs

6 egg whites

¼ cup skim milk

¼ cup plain nonfat yogurt

2 ounces bleu cheese

Fresh-cracked black pepper, to taste

1. Preheat oven to 375°F.
2. Tear the bread into large pieces. Grease a 2-quart casserole pan with the oil.
3. In a large mixing bowl, beat the whole eggs and egg whites; add the milk, yogurt, and cheese. Place the bread pieces in the prepared casserole pan, then pour in the egg mixture. Bake for 40 to 50 minutes, until the mixture is set and the top is golden brown. To serve, cut into squares and season with pepper.

Polenta

 Serves 6

1 cup skim milk

2 cups favorite stock
   (see recipes in Chapter 7)

½ cup cornmeal

¼ cup grated cheese (optional)

Fresh-cracked black pepper,
   to taste

Polenta lends itself well to the incorporation of all of your favorite ingredients. Experiment!

1. Bring the milk and stock to a boil over medium heat in a saucepan. Slowly whisk in the cornmeal a bit at a time; stir frequently until cooked, approximately 15 minutes, until mixture is the consistency of mashed potatoes. Remove from heat, add the cheese, and season with pepper.

Fruit-Stuffed French Toast

 Serves 6

Total Cost: $6.01

Calories per Serving: 336

Fat: 11.2 grams

Protein: 10 grams

Sodium: 388 mg

Carbohydrates: 50 grams

Cholesterol: 99.2 mg

½ teaspoon olive oil

3 small to medium loaves challah

2 cups seasonal fresh fruit

2 whole eggs

4 egg whites

¼ cup skim milk

1 cup orange juice

¼ cup nonfat plain yogurt

¼ cup confectioners' sugar

1. Preheat oven to 375°F. Grease a baking sheet with the oil.
2. Slice the bread into thick (2½- to 3-inch) slices with a serrated knife at a severe angle to form long bias slices (a medium-large loaf of challah will yield 3 thick bias slices). Cut a slit into the bottom crust of each slice to form a pocket.
3. Peel the fruit if necessary, then dice into large pieces and fill the pockets in the bread. Press the pocket closed.
4. In a large mixing bowl, beat the eggs and egg whites, then add the milk. Dip the bread into the egg mixture, letting it fully absorb the mixture. Place the bread on the prepared baking sheet. Bake for 10 minutes on one side, flip, and bake 10 minutes more.
5. While the bread is baking, pour the orange juice into a small saucepan; boil until reduced by half and the mixture becomes syrupy. Remove the French toast from the oven, and cut in half diagonally. Serve each with dollop of yogurt, a drizzle of juice, and a sprinkling of sugar.

Mediterranean Omelet

 Serves 6

2 whole eggs

6 egg whites

¼ cups plain nonfat yogurt

½ teaspoon extra-virgin olive oil

2 ounces lean ham

3 ounces cheese (Swiss or any other), shredded

¼ cup fresh parsley, chopped

Fresh-cracked black pepper, to taste

1. If finishing the omelet in an oven, preheat the oven to 350°F.
2. In a medium-size bowl, beat the eggs and egg whites, then whisk in the yogurt. Heat half of the oil to medium temperature in a large sauté pan. Quickly sauté the ham, then remove and drain on paper towel.
3. In the same pan, heat the remaining oil to medium temperature. Pour in the egg mixture, then sprinkle in the ham and cheese. Stir once only. Continuously move the pan over the heat, using a spatula to push the edges inward slightly to allow the egg mixture to pour outward and solidify. When the mixture is mostly solidified, use a spatula to fold it in half.
4. Cover and finish cooking on the stovetop on low heat or uncovered in an oven for approximately 5 minutes. Sprinkle with parsley and black pepper and serve.

Season the Pan

When making omelets, always make sure your pan is properly seasoned. To season a cast iron or stainless steel pan, put it on the stove top and once warm, coat the pan with oil. Afterward, carefully put the pan in a 300°F oven for 45 to 60 minutes. Remove the pan from the oven and allow it to cool to room temperature. Seasoned pans must be washed in warm water with a tiny amount of dish soap and dried immediately.

Pastina and Egg

Serves 6

💲 Total Cost: $1.99

Calories per Serving: 162

Fat: 3.3 grams

Protein: 10.1 grams

Sodium: 140.1 mg

Carbohydrates: 22.9 grams

Cholesterol: 39.3 mg

1 whole egg

2 egg whites

3 cups chicken fat-free broth

1½ cups pastina

1 ounce fresh Parmesan
cheese, grated

Fresh-cracked black pepper,
to taste

¼ cup fresh parsley, chopped

1. Beat the egg and egg whites. Bring the broth to a slow boil
   in a medium-size saucepot, then add the pastina; stir frequently until almost al dente.
2. Whisk in the eggs, stirring constantly until the eggs are
   completely cooked and the pasta is al dente. Remove from
   heat and ladle into bowls. Sprinkle in cheese, pepper, and
   parsley.

Fresh Fruit and Plain Yogurt

 Serves 6

$ Total Cost: $6.47

Calories per Serving: 211

Fat: 0.9 grams

Protein: 9 grams

Sodium: 203.2 mg

Carbohydrates: 36.9 grams

Cholesterol: 4.8 mg

¼ fresh cantaloupe

¼ fresh honeydew melon

2 fresh kiwi

1 fresh peach

1 fresh plum

½ pint fresh raspberries

6 cups plain nonfat yogurt

6 mint sprigs (tops only)

1. Slice the cantaloupe and honeydew paper-thin (use a vegetable peeler if necessary and if the fruit is not overly ripe). Slice the kiwi into ¼-inch-thick circles. Slice the peach and plum into thin wedges. Carefully rinse the raspberries.
2. Spoon the yogurt into serving bowls and arrange the fruits decoratively around each rim. (The cantaloupe and melon can be arranged like a lacy border; the other cut fruit can be fanned and placed atop the yogurt.) Sprinkle the raspberries on top. Garnish with mint.

Fruit for Breakfast

Proponents of proper food-combining say that fruit makes the best breakfast. They also suggest that you always eat fruit on an empty stomach and wait 2 hours before eating any other food. This ensures proper digestion.

Eggs in Crusty Italian Bread

 Serves 6

6 (2-inch) slices Italian bread

1 teaspoon virgin olive oil

2 red peppers, thinly sliced

½ shallot, minced

6 eggs

Fresh-cracked black pepper,
    to taste

Kosher salt, to taste

1. Cut out large circles from the center of the bread slices; discard the center pieces and set the hollowed-out bread slices aside. Heat half of the oil to medium in a sauté pan. Sauté the peppers and shallots until tender. Remove from heat and drain on paper towel; keep warm.
2. Heat the remaining oil on medium-high heat in a large sauté pan. Place the bread slices in the pan. Crack 1 egg into the hollowed-out center of each bread slice. When the eggs solidify, flip them together with the bread (being careful to keep the egg in place), and cook to desired doneness.
3. To serve, top with pepper-shallot mixture, and add pepper and salt.

Sweetened Brown Rice

 Serves 6

 Total Cost: $1.51

 Calories per Serving: 196

Fat: 2.2 grams

Protein: 4.8 grams

Sodium: 36.3 mg

Carbohydrates: 38.9 grams

Cholesterol: 0 mg

1½ cups soy milk

1½ cups water

1 cup brown rice

1 tablespoon honey

¼ teaspoon nutmeg

Fresh fruit (optional)

This recipe is perfect for a cold winter day, providing a great alternative to cold cereal.

1. Place all the ingredients except the fresh fruit in a medium-size saucepan; bring the mixture to a slow simmer and cover with a tight-fitting lid. Simmer for 45 to 60 minutes, until the rice is tender and done. Serve in bowls, topped with your favorite fresh fruit.

Inexpensive and Tasty

Why spend the extra money on packaged hot rice cereals when you can make your own less-expensive version as described in this recipe?

Creamy Sweet Risotto

Serves 6

 Total Cost: $2.40

 Calories per Serving: 251

Fat: 6.1 grams

Protein: 5.8 grams

Sodium: 40.7 mg

Carbohydrates: 44.2 grams

Cholesterol: 3.3 mg

1 teaspoon clarified butter

1 teaspoon olive oil

1 cup arborio rice

¼ cup white grape juice

2 cups skim milk

⅓ cup shredded coconut

½ cup raisins or dried currants

3 teaspoons honey

1. Heat a large sauté pan to medium temperature, then add the butter and oil. Using a wooden spoon, stir in the rice. Add the juice, stirring until completely incorporated. Add the skim milk ¼ cup at a time, stirring constantly. Make certain that each ¼ cup is fully incorporated before adding the next.
2. When the rice is completely cooked, add the coconut. Serve in bowls or on plates, sprinkled with raisins and drizzled with honey.

Israeli Couscous with Dried-Fruit Chutney

 Serves 6

$ Total Cost: $5.55

Calories per Serving: 268

Fat: 2.7 grams

Protein: 5.7 grams

Sodium: 15.4 mg

Carbohydrates: 55.3 grams

Cholesterol: 0.1 mg

CHUTNEY

¼ cup medium-diced dried dates

¼ cup medium-diced dried figs

¼ cup medium-diced dried currants

¼ cup slivered almonds

COUSCOUS

2¼ cups fresh orange juice

2¼ cups water

4½ cups couscous

1 teaspoon grated orange rind

2 tablespoons nonfat plain yogurt

1. Mix together all the chutney ingredients; set aside.
2. Bring the orange juice and water to a boil in a medium-size pot. Stir in the couscous, then add the orange rind. Remove from heat immediately, cover, and let stand for 5 minutes. Fluff the mixture with a fork.
3. Serve in bowls with a spoonful of chutney and a dollop of yogurt.

Yogurt Cheese and Fruit

 Serves 6

3 cups plain nonfat yogurt

1 teaspoon fresh lemon juice

½ cup orange juice

½ cup water

1 fresh Golden Delicious apple

1 fresh pear

¼ cup honey

¼ cup dried cranberries or raisins

This breakfast is worth the extra effort of making the yogurt cheese. If you do not have the time or inclination, use farmer cheese instead.

1. Prepare the yogurt cheese the day before by lining a colander or strainer with cheesecloth. Spoon the yogurt into the cheesecloth and place the strainer over a pot or bowl to catch the whey; refrigerate for at least 8 hours before serving. Transfer cheese to a separate container and store in the refrigerator until ready to use.
2. In a large mixing bowl, mix together the juices and water. Cut the apple and pear into wedges, and place the wedges in the juice mixture; let sit for at least 5 minutes. Strain off and discard the liquid.
3. When the yogurt is firm, remove from refrigerator, slice, and place on plates. Arrange the fruit wedges around the yogurt. Drizzle with honey and sprinkle with cranberries just before serving.

Pancetta on Baguette

 Serves 6

 Total Cost: $5.61

 Calories per Serving: 326.2

Fat: 8.4 grams

Protein: 15.8 grams

Sodium: 825.1 mg

Carbohydrates: 46.4 grams

Cholesterol: 23.7 mg

1 baguette (French bread)

½–1 teaspoon extra-virgin olive oil

6 ounces pancetta (ham, prosciutto, or Canadian bacon can be substituted)

¼ cantaloupe, medium-diced

¼ honeydew melon, medium-diced

3 ounces goat cheese

Fresh-cracked black pepper, to taste

1. Preheat broiler on medium-high heat.
2. Slice the baguette on the bias and place on baking sheet. Brush each slice with oil, then toast lightly on each side.
3. Slice the pancetta paper-thin and into thin strips, then place on top of each baguette slice. place under broiler. Cook quickly, approximately 1 minute, paying close attention to prevent burning.
4. While the baguette cooks, mix the cantaloupe and melon in a small bowl. When baguettes are done, remove them from the oven and place on a plate to serve. Sprinkle with cheese and black pepper. Garnish with a spoonful of melon mix.

Pancetta a Must

The salty spice of the pancetta is a perfect foil for the sweet fruit. Using pancetta or prosciutto is a "must" for a full appreciation of this recipe.

Vegetable Pita with Feta Cheese

Serves 6

Total Cost: $5.34

Calories per Serving: 251

Fat: 4.8 grams

Protein: 9.3 grams

Sodium: 477.4 mg

Carbohydrates: 43.9 grams

Cholesterol: 12.6 mg

1 eggplant, sliced into ½-inch pieces, lengthwise

2 zucchini, sliced into ½-inch pieces, lengthwise

1 red onion, cut into ⅓-inch rings

1 teaspoon extra-virgin olive oil

Fresh-cracked black pepper, to taste

6 whole-wheat pitas

3 ounces feta cheese

1. Preheat oven to 375°F.
2. Brush the sliced vegetables with oil and place on a rack set on a baking sheet. Sprinkle with black pepper. Roast until tender. (The vegetables can be prepared the night before and refrigerated until needed; reheat or bring to room temperature before roasting.)
3. Slice a 3-inch opening in each pita to gain access to the pocket. Toast the pitas if desired. Fill the pitas with the cooked vegetables. Add cheese to each and serve.

Almond Mascarpone Dumplings

 Serves 6

$ Total Cost: $5.22

Calories per Serving: 315

Fat: 11 grams

Protein: 11.5 grams

Sodium: 50.9 mg

Carbohydrates: 45.4 grams

Cholesterol: 12.3 mg

1 cup whole-wheat flour

1 cup all-purpose unbleached flour

¼ cup ground almonds

4 egg whites

3 ounces mascarpone cheese

1 teaspoon extra-virgin olive oil

2 teaspoons apple juice

1 tablespoon butter

¼ cup honey

1. Sift together both types of flour in a large bowl. Mix in the almonds. In a separate bowl, cream together the egg whites, cheese, oil, and juice on medium speed with an electric mixer.
2. Combine the flour and egg white mixture with a dough hook on medium speed or by hand until a dough forms.
3. Boil 1 gallon water in a medium-size saucepot. Take a spoonful of the dough and use a second spoon to push it into the boiling water. Cook until the dumpling floats to the top, about 5 to 10 minutes. You can cook several dumplings at once; just take care not to crowd the pot. Remove with a slotted spoon and drain on paper towels.
4. Heat a medium-size sauté pan on medium-high heat. Add the butter, then place the dumplings in the pan and cook until light brown. Place on serving plates and drizzle with honey.

Multigrain Toast with Grilled Vegetables

 Serves 6

 Total Cost: $4.83

 Calories per Serving: 195

Fat: 6.9 grams

Protein: 6 grams

Sodium: 255.9 mg

Carbohydrates: 24.1 grams

Cholesterol: 11.1 mg

½ eggplant

½ zucchini

½ yellow squash

½ red pepper

½ yellow pepper

½ green pepper

1 teaspoon extra-virgin olive oil

6 multigrain bread slices

3 ounces goat cheese

¼ cup fresh marjoram, chopped after measuring

Fresh-cracked black pepper, to taste

1. Slice the eggplant, zucchini, and squash in 3-inch lengths, and then cut each of those pieces ¼- to ½-inch thick. Cut the peppers in half. Preheat a grill to medium heat. Brush the vegetables with the oil and grill all until fork tender. Cut all the vegetables into a large dice. (Vegetables can be prepared the night before and refrigerated; reheat or bring to room temperature before serving.)
2. Grill the bread until lightly toasted, then remove from heat and top with vegetables. Sprinkle with cheese, marjoram, and black pepper.

Grilled Vegetables

As you can see, many of the recipes in this book use grilled vegetables. When preparing roasted or grilled vegetables for dinner or any meal, always make double the quantity. Refrigerate the extra portion and use it the next day in your breakfast or lunch meal. Grilling vegetables brings out the sweet flavor. Use any seasonal vegetables.

The $7 a Meal Mediterranean Cookbook

Cinnamon-Nutmeg Polenta with Dried Fruit and Nuts

 Serves 10

 Total Cost: $2.40

 Calories per Serving: 360

Fat: 15.7 grams

Protein: 5.2 grams

Sodium: 22.5 mg

Carbohydrates: 52.5 grams

Cholesterol: 36.4 mg

1½ cups cornmeal

½ cup brown sugar (optional)

1 tablespoon cinnamon (preferably freshly ground)

½ teaspoon ground nutmeg

4 cups water

1 cup whole milk

2 tablespoons unsalted butter

1 cup heavy cream (or substitute plain yogurt)

½ cup honey

½ cup finely chopped pecans or walnuts

½ cup raisins or other dried fruit of choice

1. Sift together the cornmeal, brown sugar, cinnamon, and nutmeg.
2. Bring the water, milk, and butter to a simmer over medium to medium-high heat in a large saucepan. Slowly whisk in the cornmeal mixture, stirring constantly to avoid lumps. Reduce heat to low. Cook for 20 to 25 minutes, uncovered and stirring frequently, until thick and creamy.
3. If using heavy cream, reduce by half the volume in a large sauté pan.
4. Spoon out the polenta into individual servings and drizzle with the cream or yogurt and honey. Sprinkle with the nuts and raisins, and serve.

CHAPTER 3
APPETIZERS

Fresh Mozzarella

Serves 4

Total Cost: $1.75

Calories per Serving: 70

Fat: 5 grams

Protein: 6 grams

Sodium: 50 mg

Carbohydrates: 0 grams

Cholesterol: 10 mg

2 gallons water

¼ cup kosher salt

1 pound mozzarella cheese
curd (can be purchased at a
specialty food store)

1. Mix the water with the salt in a large saucepot and bring to
   a slow simmer. While the water comes to a simmer, thinly
   slice or grate the mozzarella curd.
2. Place the curd in the simmering water, stir with a wooden
   spoon, and remove from heat. Stir every few minutes until
   the curd begins to form a ball and stretches when stirred.
   Continue to stir for approximately 5 to 10 minutes, then let it
   sit for 15 minutes or until the curd and whey fully separate.
3. Using a slotted spoon, transfer the curd to a colander lined
   with cheesecloth and let the whey drain from the curd mixture. Press the curd again to remove any remaining whey.
   Continue pressing until it is just cool enough (but still hot) to
   knead into a ball with your hands. While the cheese is still
   hot, stretch it and fold it back onto itself; repeat this until
   it will not stretch any more. When it begins to stretch like
   taffy, it is almost done. Mold into a ball or string or desired
   shape. You can serve it immediately at room temperature
   or wrap it in plastic wrap, refrigerate, and serve later. It will
   keep for up to a month refrigerated.

Having Difficulty?
If you are having difficulty
shredding the cheese, put it
in the freezer for a few minutes. When you take it out it
will be much more workable.

Oven-Dried Tomatoes

 Serves 6

 Total Cost: $2.32

Calories per Serving: 24

Fat: 0.2 grams

Protein: 1 grams

Sodium: 53 mg

Carbohydrates: 5.3 grams

Cholesterol: 0 mg

6 plum tomatoes

3 cloves garlic

¼ cup fresh basil

Fresh-cracked black pepper,
  to taste

Kosher salt, to taste

1. Preheat oven to 200°F.
2. Cut the tomatoes into ⅓-inch-thick slices. Lay out slices in a single layer on a sheet pan. Mince the garlic, and finely chop the basil. Sprinkle the tomatoes with the garlic, basil, black pepper, and salt.
3. Dry in the oven for approximately 8 hours. Then remove and serve on top of Flatbread (see recipe in Chapter 11).

Smoked Trout Hors d'Oeuvres

 Serves 6

$ Total Cost: $6.63

Calories per Serving: 291

Fat: 8 grams

Protein: 20.8 grams

Sodium: 1625 mg

Carbohydrates: 33.2 grams

Cholesterol: 22.7 mg

¾ pound smoked trout

12 slices French bread

¼ cup fresh chives

1 fresh plum tomato

3 ounces provolone cheese

Fresh-cracked black pepper, to taste

1 teaspoon extra-virgin olive oil

1. Remove the skin and bone from the trout, then gently flake the trout with a fork. Lightly toast the bread. Chop the chives and finely chop the tomato. Grate the cheese.
2. Mound a small spoonful of trout on each piece of toast and place on a serving platter. Carefully top with provolone, then sprinkle with chopped tomatoes. Shake chives over the top of each. Sprinkle pepper over each one and drizzle with oil before serving.

Stuffed Grape Leaves

 Serves 6

Total Cost: $2.90

Calories per Serving: 140

Fat: 3.9 grams

Protein: 4.6 grams

Sodium: 1198.7 mg

Carbohydrates: 22.7 grams

Cholesterol: 8.4 mg

1 small jar grape leaves

1 leek

¼ cup fresh oregano

2 ounces feta cheese

1 teaspoon extra-virgin
olive oil

1 cup uncooked white rice

2 cups Basic Vegetable Stock
(see recipe in Chapter 7)

Fresh-cracked black pepper,
to taste

1. Drain, rinse, and separate the grape leaves. Finely mince the leek and mince the oregano. Crumble the cheese.
2. Heat the oil to medium temperature in a medium-size saucepan, then add the leeks and toss them in the oil. Add the rice and quickly toss again. Pour in the stock and stir. Cover and cook for approximately 15 to 20 minutes, until the rice is thoroughly cooked.
3. Cool the rice in a medium-size mixing bowl, then add the feta, pepper, and oregano.
4. Lay out a grape leaf. Place a spoonful of the rice mixture on the center of the grape leaf, then fold each end over the other and seal tightly. Repeat until all the grape leaves and rice mixture are used. Serve on a platter.

Vegetable Kabobs

 Serves 6

 Total Cost: $4.88

Calories per Serving: 45.3

Fat: 2.5 grams

Protein: 1.4 grams

Sodium: 52.2 mg

Carbohydrates: 5 grams

Cholesterol: 0 mg

12 scallions

1 large red pepper

1 large yellow pepper

1 large green pepper

12 large button mushrooms

1 tablespoon olive oil

Fresh-cracked black pepper, to taste

Kosher salt, to taste

Serving kabobs as an appetizer at parties is a good idea because guests can easily handle the food without using cutlery.

1. Cut standard wooden skewers in half for appetizer-size portions, then soak the skewers in water for a minimum of 1 hour.
2. Preheat grill or broiler.
3. Trim off the roots and dark green parts of the scallions. Dice the peppers into large pieces.
4. Thread the vegetables onto the skewers, and brush all sides of the vegetables with oil. Season with pepper and salt.
5. Place the skewers on the grill or under the broiler, paying close attention as they cook, as they can easily burn. Cook until the vegetables are fork tender.

Soaking the Skewers

When using wooden skewers in cooking, always soak them in water for an hour before spearing the food items. Soaking the skewers allows you to place them on the grill for a time without them burning.

Fresh Herb Dip with Eggplant

 Yields 2 cups

Total Cost: $0.62

Calories per Serving: 20

Fat: 0.9 grams

Protein: 0.7 grams

Sodium: 21.3 mg

Carbohydrates: 2.4 grams

Cholesterol: 0.2 mg

1 large eggplant

3 cloves garlic

1 tablespoon olive oil

½ cup Yogurt Cheese (see recipe in this chapter)

1 tablespoon each fresh parsley, basil, and rosemary

Fresh-ground black pepper, to taste

Kosher salt, to taste

1. Slice the eggplant in half lengthwise and mince the garlic. Brush the cut side of the eggplant with the oil, sprinkle with garlic, and roast on foil in oven preheated to 375°F or place on the grill for 10 minutes. Place in a plastic bag for 5 minutes (the steam in the bag will help loosen the skin), then remove the skin if desired.
2. Spoon the eggplant pulp into a blender, and pulse. Add the yogurt cheese ¼ cup at a time, and blend until it reaches the consistency of a thick sauce. Add the herbs, pepper, and salt, and stir to combine.
3. Refrigerate for at least 2 hours before serving.

Chicken Meatballs with Apple Chutney

 Serves 6

 Total Cost: $3.34

 Calories per Serving: 256

Fat: 15.1 grams

Protein: 20 grams

Sodium: 163.8 mg

Carbohydrates: 11.6 grams

Cholesterol: 116.6 mg

Olive oil

2 slices toasted Italian bread

1 pound ground chicken

¼ cup dried cranberries

¼ cup chopped pecans

1 egg

¼ teaspoon cinnamon

¼ teaspoon curry powder

Pinch of kosher salt

Fresh-cracked black pepper, to taste

½ cup Apple Chutney (see recipe in Chapter 5)

1. Preheat oven to 350°F. Brush a baking dish with oil.
2. Soak the bread in water and then squeeze out the liquid. Mix the soaked bread and all the remaining ingredients except the apple chutney in a bowl. Shape the mixture into small balls. Place the balls in the prepared baking dish. Cover with foil and bake for about 20 minutes. Serve with apple chutney.

Artist at Work

Always keep a pastry brush or a small natural bristle paintbrush handy as one of your basic kitchen tools. They are great for getting just the right amount of oil in a pan or for brushing food with a light coating of oil before cooking.

Haddock Fish Cakes

Serves 6

 Total Cost: $6.62

 Calories per Serving: 144

Fat: 3.5 grams

Protein: 22.7 grams

Sodium: 100.6 mg

Carbohydrates: 4.7 grams

Cholesterol: 63.4 mg

1 pound haddock

2 leeks

1 red pepper

2 egg whites

Pinch of kosher salt

Fresh-cracked black pepper,
    to taste

1 tablespoon olive oil

1. Finely shred the raw fish with a fork. Dice the leeks and
   red pepper. Combine all the ingredients except the oil in a
   medium-size bowl; mix well. Form the mixture into small
   oval patties.
2. Heat the oil in a medium-size sauté pan. Place the cakes in
   the pan and loosely cover with the lid; sauté the cakes for
   4 to 6 minutes on each side. Drain on a rack covered with
   paper towels; serve immediately.

Lamb Patties

 Serves 6

$ Total Cost: $2.53

Calories per Serving: 160

Fat: 9.8 grams

Protein: 11.4 grams

Sodium: 87.8 mg

Carbohydrates: 6.9 grams

Cholesterol: 36.6 mg

1 shallot

2 cloves garlic

½ pound ground lamb

1 egg white

¼ cup dried currants

¼ cup pistachio nuts

½ teaspoon ground cinnamon

Fresh-cracked black pepper, to taste

Pinch of kosher salt

The lamb can be served rare to medium-rare, but the egg must be thoroughly cooked. Fruit chutneys are a nice accompaniment with meat patties (see chutney recipes in Chapter 5).

1. Preheat oven to 350°F.
2. Peel and mince the shallot and garlic; mix with the lamb, egg white, currants, nuts, and cinnamon. Season with pepper and salt.
3. Form the mixture into small ovals. Place them in a baking dish and bake for approximately 15 minutes.

Marinated Portobello Mushrooms

 Serves 6

$ Total Cost: $3.72

Calories per Serving: 31

Fat: 0.9 grams

Protein: 2.1 grams

Sodium: 44.3 mg

Carbohydrates: 4.8 grams

Cholesterol: 0 mg

6 portobello mushrooms

1 teaspoon extra-virgin olive oil

2 teaspoons balsamic vinegar

Pinch of iodized salt

Fresh-cracked black pepper, to taste

¼ cup fresh marjoram, chopped after measuring

¼ cup fresh oregano, chopped after measuring

Portobello mushrooms have such a meaty flavor, they can be used in place of meat in many recipes.

1. Preheat oven to 400°F.
2. Remove the stems from the caps of the mushrooms and scrape out the black membrane. Slice the stems in half.
3. Mix together the remaining ingredients. Combine the caps and stems with the marinade in a container (plastic tub or sealable bag); marinate for at least 3 hours.
4. Roast the mushrooms for 15 to 20 minutes on oven rack. Cut the caps into small wedges and serve.

Shredded Vegetable Patties

 Serves 6

$ Total Cost: $2.84

Calories per Serving: 113

Fat: 5.2 grams

Protein: 6 grams

Sodium: 195 mg

Carbohydrates: 11.3 grams

Cholesterol: 8.3 mg

2 carrots

2 small zucchini

1 red onion

3 stalks celery

1 egg white

2 tablespoons all-purpose flour

2 ounces Romano cheese

1 tablespoon olive oil

Fresh-cracked black pepper, to taste

1. Finely shred all the vegetables and mix them with the egg white, flour, and cheese in a medium-size bowl. Form the mixture into small ovals.
2. Heat the oil to medium temperature in a sauté pan. Place the patties in the oil and sauté until lightly golden brown. Turn the patties over and sauté the other side until golden brown.
3. Drain on a rack covered with paper towels. Add pepper, to taste, and serve with your favorite sauce as an accompaniment.

Garlic-Parsley Yogurt Cheese

Serves 6

$ Total Cost: $3.41

Calories per Serving: 93

Fat: 0.3 grams

Protein: 5 grams

Sodium: 118.3 mg

Carbohydrates: 13.4 grams

Cholesterol: 3.0 mg

32 ounces nonfat plain yogurt

½ bulb garlic, minced

Fresh-cracked black pepper,
   to taste

½ cup fresh parsley, minced
   after measuring

Making yogurt cheese requires overnight refrigeration. The fresh flavor of the yogurt produces an equally light cheese, which has many uses.

1. Mix together all the ingredients. Place the mixture in a colander lined with cheesecloth, then place the colander in a large bowl to catch the whey. Refrigerate overnight. When you are ready to serve, remove the cheese from the colander and dispose of the whey and cheesecloth. Slice and serve.

Olive Cheese Bread

 Serves 6

¼ pound pitted cured olives

1 clove garlic

2 tablespoons pine nuts

1½ tablespoons olive oil

1 long loaf crusty bread

¼ pound Gorgonzola cheese

1. Process the olives, garlic, pine nuts, and olive oil as finely as possible. Slice the bread into ¼-inch-thick slices. Spread the olive mixture on the bread and top with Gorgonzola. Serve as is or flash cook under broiler until the cheese begins to bubble.

Eggplant Bruschetta

Serves 6

$ Total Cost: $4.93

Calories per Serving: 229

Fat: 11 grams

Protein: 5.6 grams

Sodium: 325.6 mg

Carbohydrates: 27.7 grams

Cholesterol: 0 mg

1 baguette (French bread), sliced into ¼-inch rounds

½ cup olive oil

5 or 6 cloves garlic, peeled (2 cloves left whole for rubbing, 3 or 4 minced for eggplant mixture)

1 medium eggplant

2 tablespoons red wine vinegar

2 tablespoons minced capers (optional)

1 teaspoon salt

1 roasted red bell pepper, peeled and diced

¼ cup fresh parsley, chopped after measuring

1. Preheat oven to 350°F. Lay the baguette rounds on an ungreased cookie sheet. Brush both sides with olive oil and set aside the rest of the oil. Toast rounds in the oven until lightly browned; then turn and toast the other side. Remove from oven. Rub one side of each warm toast with garlic; set aside.

2. Place a piece of aluminum foil on the bottom oven rack. Prick eggplant all over with a fork. Place the eggplant directly on top oven rack and bake for about 1 hour, until tender. Test tenderness by inserting a fork into the flesh of the eggplant. If the fork slides easily in and out, the egg-plant is tender. Remove from oven and let the eggplant cool enough to handle. Cut the eggplant in half and scoop the flesh into a bowl. Discard skin and stem.

3. Mince 3 or 4 cloves of the garlic, according to your taste, and add to cooked eggplant along with ¼ cup olive oil, red wine vinegar, capers, and salt. Mix thoroughly.

4. Spread each toast with eggplant mixture. Top with diced roasted red bell pepper, and sprinkle with parsley.

Hummus

 Serves 6

$ Total Cost: $1.08

Calories per Serving: 70

Fat: 2 grams

Protein: 2.3 grams

Sodium: 120.9 mg

Carbohydrates: 11.3 grams

Cholesterol: 0 mg

1 lemon

¼ cup fresh parsley

1 cup chickpeas (or other type of white bean), cooked

6 cloves roasted garlic (for instructions, see Roasted Garlic Served on Crostini recipe on the next page)

2 teaspoons extra-virgin olive oil

Fresh-cracked black pepper, to taste

Kosher salt or sea salt, to taste (optional)

For a tasty variation of traditional hummus, sprinkle toasted sesame seeds over the top; they provide a nice little crunch and a slight tahini flavor.

1. Zest and juice the lemon. Chop the parsley.
2. In a blender, purée the cooked chickpeas, then add the roasted garlic, lemon zest, and juice. Continue to purée until the mixture is thoroughly combined. Drizzle in the olive oil in a stream while continuing to purée until all the oil is incorporated and the mixture is smooth. Remove the mixture from the blender and season with pepper and salt, if desired. Adjust seasonings to taste. Before serving, sprinkle with chopped parsley.

Traditional Hummus

Traditional hummus is made with chickpeas, which are also known as "garbanzo beans," but this appetizer can be prepared with many different beans. Hummus can be used as a dip, spread, sauce, or topping.

Roasted Garlic Served on Crostini

Serves 6

$ Total Cost: $1.51

Calories per Serving: 162

Fat: 5.2 grams

Protein: 4.9 grams

Sodium: 249.3 mg

Carbohydrates: 24 grams

Cholesterol: 0 mg

1 whole bulb garlic

2 tablespoons virgin olive oil

½ cup fresh parsley

½ baguette (French bread)

1. Preheat oven to 375°F.
2. Cut off the top quarter of the garlic bulb. Rub both cut sides of garlic with some of the olive oil, then place the top back on the bulb and wrap in foil. Place in the oven and bake until the cloves are fork tender (the same tenderness as a baked potato), about 5 to 10 minutes.
3. While the garlic cooks, chop the parsley. To make the crostini, slice the baguette thinly on the bias. Brush with remaining oil and place on a baking sheet. Toast until light brown.
4. Serve the bulb intact on a platter surrounded by crostini and sprinkled with parsley.

Spreading the Garlic
To create a spread from the bulb of garlic, cut the bulb in half with a serrated knife. Once the cloves are exposed, scoop them out with a spoon and transfer into a bowl. Mash the cloves with a fork and spread onto the crostini.

The $7 a Meal Mediterranean Cookbook

Tomato, Mozzarella, and Basil

 Serves 4

$ Total Cost: $5.45

Calories per Serving: 266

Fat: 23 grams

Protein: 10.4 grams

Sodium: 270.5 mg

Carbohydrates: 5.3 grams

Cholesterol: 33.3 mg

6 ripe red tomatoes

6 ounces fresh mozzarella
cheese (see Fresh Mozza-
rella recipe in this chapter)

10 fresh basil leaves

¼ cup olive oil

1. Slice tomatoes and mozzarella.
2. Stack the basil leaves, roll them up, and slice them into ribbons.
3. On a platter, alternate layers of tomatoes and mozzarella, drizzle with olive oil, and sprinkle with basil.

Pork and Apple Meatballs

 Serves 10

Total Cost: $4.40

Calories per Serving: 344

Fat: 21.1 grams

Protein: 21.5 grams

Sodium: 184.2 mg

Carbohydrates: 16.7 grams

Cholesterol: 81.9 mg

1 tablespoon olive oil

5 thick slices day-old or
    toasted Italian bread

1 yellow onion

3 tart apples

2 sprigs fresh oregano

2 pounds lean ground pork

1 egg, lightly beaten

¾ cup chopped walnuts

Fresh-cracked black pepper,
    to taste

1. Preheat oven to 375°F. Lightly grease a baking sheet with the oil. Soak the bread in water for 1 minute. Thoroughly squeeze out all the liquid. Peel and finely chop the onion. Peel and finely dice the apples. Clean and chop the oregano leaves.
2. In a large mixing bowl, thoroughly combine all the ingredients. Form the mixture into 2-inch balls.
3. Place the meatballs on the prepared baking sheet. Bake for about 30 minutes, until thoroughly cooked and golden brown.
4. Transfer the meatballs to paper towels to drain. Serve as desired.

Turkey and Fig Balls

 Serves 10

Total Cost: $5.79

Calories per Serving: 354

Fat: 17.4 grams

Protein: 28.7 grams

Sodium: 270.5 mg

Carbohydrates: 19.9 grams

Cholesterol: 113.6 mg

5 thick slices day-old or toasted Italian bread

½ cup dried figs

1 yellow onion

2 sprigs fresh sage or 1 tablespoon dried sage

2 pounds ground turkey

1 egg, lightly beaten

½ cup chopped pecans

Fresh-cracked black pepper, to taste

1. Soak the bread in water for 1 minute. Thoroughly squeeze out all the liquid. Finely chop the figs. Peel and dice the onion. Clean and chop the sage leaves (if using fresh sage).
2. In a large mixing bowl, thoroughly combine all the ingredients. Form the mixture into balls about 2 to 3 inches in size.
3. Bake or fry the meatballs: To bake, preheat oven to 375°F. Place the meatballs in a lightly greased baking pan, and cover. Bake for 30 minutes. Uncover, and brown for 5 to 10 minutes. To fry, heat about 1 tablespoon olive oil to medium temperature in a skillet. Fry for 30 minutes, uncovered and stirring occasionally, until cooked through.
4. Transfer the meatballs to paper towels to drain. Serve plain, with sauce, or over pasta.

Flatbread with Olive Tapénade

Serves 6

FLATBREAD (CHAPTER 11)

½ cup all-purpose flour

½ cup whole-wheat flour

¼ teaspoon iodized salt

½ cup water

TAPÉNADE

1½-2 bulbs roasted garlic (for roasting instructions, see Roasted Garlic Served on Crostini in this chapter)

½ cup kalamata olives (pitted)

Fresh-cracked black pepper, to taste

1. Sift together the flours and salt. Add water and mix on medium-low speed with dough hook or by hand until completely incorporated. Place in a bowl and cover loosely with plastic wrap. Let the dough rest in refrigerator for at least 1 hour.
2. Roll out the dough to ¼-inch thickness and cut into a 3-inch circle.
3. Heat a medium-size sauté pan to medium-high temperature. Place the flatbread dough in the sauté pan and cook for 3 minutes on each side, until golden brown.
4. Using a food processor or blender, purée the garlic, olives, and black pepper. To serve, spread the tapénade onto the flatbread.

Flatbread Varieties

Flatbread can be used in a variety of ways. In addition to serving it with tapénade, flatbread can be dipped into sauces and used to make sandwiches. Every culture has its own version of flatbread, from Mexican tortillas to Chinese scallion pancakes.

Bruschetta with Marinated Red Pepper

Serves 6

 Total Cost: $3.10

 Calories per Serving: 204

Fat: 4.8 grams

Protein: 8.1 grams

Sodium: 439.9 mg

Carbohydrates: 31.1 grams

Cholesterol: 6.2 mg

3 red peppers

1 teaspoon extra-virgin olive oil

1 teaspoon balsamic vinegar

¼ cup fresh oregano, chopped

12 (1½-inch-thick) slices baguette (French bread)

1½ ounces Manchego cheese (Romano or Parmesan can be substituted)

Fresh-cracked black pepper, to taste

1. Preheat oven to 400°F.
2. Coat the whole peppers with a bit of the oil and place on a baking sheet; roast until the skin blisters, approximately 10 minutes. Remove the peppers from the oven and immediately place in a plastic bag; let sit for a minimum of 5 minutes. Remove the peppers from the bag and peel off and discard the skin. Purée the peppers in a blender, then add the vinegar and continue to process into a smooth paste. Mix in the chopped oregano. Let stand for at least 1 hour (can be prepared a day in advance and refrigerated).
3. Use a pastry brush to coat the bread slices lightly with the remaining oil. Toast until lightly golden brown.
4. Spread the puréed pepper on the toasted bread and sprinkle with cheese and black pepper.

Sesame Cheese Puffs

Serves 6

Total Cost: $2.84

Calories per Serving: 258

Fat: 19.4 grams

Protein: 11 grams

Sodium: 324.8 mg

Carbohydrates: 10.2 grams

Cholesterol: 89 mg

4 tablespoons sesame seeds,
   plus extra for coating

½ cup flour

½ teaspoon baking powder

Fresh-cracked black pepper,
   to taste

2 egg whites

2 egg yolks

3 ounces Parmesan cheese,
   grated

¼ cup fontina cheese, grated

Olive oil for frying

1. Preheat oven to 350°F.
2. Spread the 4 tablespoons of sesame seeds on a baking pan and toast lightly in the oven, about 5 minutes.
3. Combine the flour, baking powder, and pepper. Beat the egg whites until stiff. In a separate bowl, beat the egg yolks and mix in the grated cheeses and toasted seeds. Combine the yolk and flour mixtures, then fold into the whites.
4. Line a sheet pan with parchment paper or foil. Form the mixture into balls by rounded spoonfuls, or pipe with a pastry bag; coat the balls with sesame seeds. Chill until firm, about 30 minutes.
5. Fry in a large skillet with 1 inch of olive oil until golden; drain on a rack covered with paper towels. Serve with a sauce of your choice.

Dates and Parmesan

 Serves 6

$ Total Cost: $6.38
Calories per Serving: 288
Fat: 5.5 grams
Protein: 8.6 grams
Sodium: 289.1 mg
Carbohydrates: 56.6 grams
Cholesterol: 6.5 mg

20 fresh dates, whole
4-ounce piece of Parmesan
    cheese

1. Pit the dates (if they have seeds) by making a lengthwise slit
   and prying out the pit.
2. Shave slices of Parmesan with a vegetable peeler. They will
   curl and be irregularly shaped.
3. Arrange pitted dates and shaved Parmesan beside each
   other on a plate.

Eggplant Roulades

Serves 6

 Total Cost: $4.71

Calories per Serving: 193

Fat: 6.9 grams

Protein: 12 grams

Sodium: 207.7 mg

Carbohydrates: 22.2 grams

Cholesterol: 19.9 mg

2 small, thin Italian eggplants

1 teaspoon olive oil

¼ cup all-purpose flour

2 egg whites

¼ cup bread crumbs

¼ cup nonfat plain yogurt

½ cup low-fat ricotta

4 ounces part-skim mozzarella cheese, shredded

1½ tablespoons grated Romano cheese

¼ cup fresh oregano, chopped

Fresh-cracked black pepper, to taste

1 cup tomato sauce (see recipes in Chapter 5)

The roulades can be fastened with toothpicks or small skewers to hold them together. Remember to soak the skewers in water first.

1. Preheat oven to 375°F.
2. Slice the eggplants into thin slices lengthwise. Pour the oil in the bottom of a baking dish. Dip the eggplant slices in the flour, then in the egg whites, then in the bread crumbs; place in oiled baking dish. Bake for approximately 3 minutes on each side until golden brown.
3. While the eggplant cooks, mix together the yogurt, cheeses, oregano, and black pepper. When the eggplant is cooked, remove from oven and drain on rack. Then spread some of the cheese mixture on one side of each eggplant slice and roll up.
4. Coat the bottom of the baking dish with tomato sauce and place the rolled eggplant slices inside the dish, letting some of the sauce come up the sides of the eggplant rolls. Lightly spoon more sauce over the top. Bake for approximately 10 minutes.

Herbed Goat Cheese and Black Olive Cucumber Cups

 Serves 6

$ Total Cost: $6.54

Calories per Serving: 185

Fat: 14.7 grams

Protein: 9.7 grams

Sodium: 384.9 mg

Carbohydrates: 3.8 grams

Cholesterol: 33.4 mg

2 cucumbers, seedless variety

9 ounces herbed and seasoned goat cheese crumbles

1 4-ounce can pitted black California olives, drained and medium diced

2 tablespoons chopped fresh parsley, plus extra for garnish

2 tablespoons julienned fresh basil

Fresh-cracked black pepper, to taste

1. To prepare the cucumbers, rinse under cool running water and pat dry. Trim off and discard about 1 inch from each end of both cucumbers (the ends are often bitter). You can either peel the cucumbers entirely or "stripe" them by leaving alternating strips of green peel.
2. Prepare 12 cucumber cups by cutting the cucumbers into slices about 1 to 1¼ inches thick; use a melon baller to scoop out the center of each slice, about three-fourths of the way down. Place the cups upside down in a single layer on paper towels for about 10 minutes before using.
3. Combine the goat cheese crumbles, olives, parsley, basil, and pepper in a medium-sized mixing bowl; toss with a fork until just combined.
4. To assemble, arrange the cups on a serving platter. Use a teaspoon to fill each cup with the goat cheese mixture until nicely mounded on the top. Garnish with chopped parsley and serve.

CHAPTER 4

LUNCH

Open-Faced Grilled Cheese

 Serves 6

 Total Cost: $3.30

Calories per Serving: 227

Fat: 11.2 grams

Protein: 10.6 grams

Sodium: 273.5 mg

Carbohydrates: 21.6 grams

Cholesterol: 26.2 mg

6 large slices raisin-pumpernickel bread

1 tablespoon extra-virgin olive oil

1 pear

1 teaspoon lemon juice

1 cup water

6 thick slices Swiss cheese (1 ounce each)

Kosher salt, to taste

Fresh-cracked black pepper, to taste

1. Preheat the oven to 350°F. Brush the bread with the oil and toast lightly.
2. Preheat broiler. Dice the pear and toss it in the lemon juice and water; drain thoroughly.
3. Place the cheese on the bread, sprinkle with diced pears, and season with salt and pepper.
4. Place under broiler until the cheese melts and the pears brown slightly, approximately 2 minutes.

Warm Open-Faced Turkey Sandwich

 Serves 6

½ baguette (French bread)

1 yellow onion

2 stalks celery

½ cup mushrooms

1 tablespoon olive oil

6 ounces turkey Demi-Glacé Reduction Sauce (see recipe in Chapter 5)

2 ounces warm turkey

Fresh-cracked black pepper, to taste

Kosher salt, to taste

1. Slice the baguette in half lengthwise. Slice the onion and finely slice the celery and mushrooms.
2. Heat the oil to medium temperature in a small saucepan, then add the onions, celery, and mushrooms. Cover and simmer at medium-low heat until the vegetables are wilted.
3. Heat the demi-glacé. Place the cooked vegetables on the baguette and layer with warm turkey.
4. To serve, cut into 6 portions and ladle demi-glacé on each.

Substituting Meat

For most of these recipes, you can substitute the meat that is called for with another meat of your choice. However, keep in mind that while some meats can be served rare or medium-rare, such as lamb, others need to be thoroughly cooked, such as chicken.

Vegetable Pita

 Serves 6

$ Total Cost: $5.22

Calories per Serving: 271

Fat: 6.5 grams

Protein: 8.2 grams

Sodium: 391.5 mg

Carbohydrates: 45.7 grams

Cholesterol: 0 mg

1 large red onion

1 large head lettuce (any type)

6 large pitas

¾ cup Hummus (see recipe in Chapter 3)

4½ cups vegetables of your choice, roasted

2 tablespoons extra-virgin olive oil

1. Thinly slice the onion and shred the lettuce. Spread hummus on each pita. Layer with onion, lettuce, and roasted vegetables. Drizzle with olive oil.

Wilted Arugula on Flatbread

 Serves 6

$ Total Cost: $2.78

Calories per Serving: 175.4

Fat: 1.7 grams

Protein: 7.2 grams

Sodium: 407.1 mg

Carbohydrates: 32 grams

Cholesterol: 4.2 mg

1 teaspoon olive oil

2 ounces pancetta

3 cups fresh arugula

12 slices Flatbread (see recipe
in Chapter 11)

Fresh-cracked black pepper,
to taste

You can use slices of extra-crispy bacon in place of the
pancetta.

1. Heat the oil to medium temperature in a medium-size
saucepan. Add the pancetta; brown. Add the arugula, allow
to wilt, and then immediately mound the mixture on the flatbread. Serve with Gorgonzola or your favorite cheese.

Caesar Sandwich

 Serves 6

 Total Cost: $5.97

Calories per Serving: 375

Fat: 23.7 grams

Protein: 10.4 grams

Sodium: 519.5 mg

Carbohydrates: 30 grams

Cholesterol: 44.1 mg

3 cloves roasted garlic (see instructions in the Roasted Garlic Served on Crostini recipe in Chapter 3)

1 anchovy fillet (optional)

1 ounce pasteurized egg yolks

½ teaspoon dry mustard

Fresh-cracked black pepper, to taste

½ cup extra-virgin olive oil

1 large head romaine lettuce

6 slices crusty Italian bread

2 ounces Parmesan cheese, grated

You must purchase pasteurized egg yolks to prevent possible salmonella poisoning.

1. Prepare the dressing by mashing together the garlic and anchovy (if using). Add the yolks, mustard, and pepper. Slowly whisk in the olive oil.
2. Clean and dry the lettuce, then toss the lettuce with the dressing.
3. Place on bread and sprinkle with Parmesan.

Watercress Sandwich

Serves 6

$ Total Cost: $4.56

Calories per Serving: 131

Fat: 4.9 grams

Protein: 6.1 grams

Sodium: 315.4 mg

Carbohydrates: 15.7 grams

Cholesterol: 14.2 mg

6 slices marble (rye-pumper-
nickel mix) bread

3 ounces Brie cheese

3 cups watercress leaves

1. Lightly toast the bread; let cool. Spread each slice with
   the Brie.
2. Clean and lay out the watercress leaves on 3 slices, then
   top with the remaining 3 slices. Cut each sandwich into 6
   small pieces. Serve 3 each with Roasted-Beet Slaw (Chapter
   6) or Pumpkin Soup (Chapter 8).

Diet Breads
For those of you watching
your weight or counting
calories, you may want to
try out some of the fat-free
or low-calorie breads available in the market. Most are
just as tasty, and you probably won't be able to tell
the difference.

Greek Pita

 Serves 6

$ Total Cost: $4.89

Calories per Serving: 253

Fat: 6.3 grams

Protein: 8.8 grams

Sodium: 518.7 mg

Carbohydrates: 40.6 grams

Cholesterol: 13.7 mg

2 European cucumbers

1 large red onion

¼ cup fresh oregano

2 anchovy fillets (optional)

6 pitas

3 ounces feta cheese

1 tablespoon olive oil

Fresh-cracked black pepper, to taste

1. Peel and dice the cucumbers and thinly slice the onion. Chop the oregano. Mash the anchovy fillets (if using).
2. Cut a slit into each pita and stuff with cucumber, onion, oregano, and feta.
3. Drizzle with oil and sprinkle with mashed anchovy and black pepper.

Curried Chicken on Lavash

 Serves 6

Total Cost: $4.37

Calories per Serving: 226

Fat: 7.2 grams

Protein: 21 grams

Sodium: 95.6 mg

Carbohydrates: 19.9 grams

Cholesterol: 48 mg

CURRIED CHICKEN

1 medium-size yellow onion

3 cloves garlic

1 carrot

1 tablespoon olive oil

¾ pound boneless chicken breast, cubed

2 tablespoons curry powder

¼ teaspoon red pepper flakes

Fresh-cracked black pepper, to taste

½ cup Chicken Stock (see recipe in Chapter 7)

LAVASH

1 cup whole-wheat flour

¼ cup water

Pinch of iodized salt

1 tablespoon olive oil

1. To prepare the chicken, peel and chop the onion, garlic, and carrot. Heat the oil to medium temperature in a saucepan. Sauté the vegetables, then add the chicken, curry powder, red pepper flakes, black pepper, and stock. Simmer for 1 hour.
2. While the chicken cooks, prepare the lavash. Mix together the flour, water, and salt with a dough hook or by hand. Heat the oil to medium temperature in a sauté pan. Divide dough into six equal pieces. Roll the lavash into 1-inch-thick disks and cook each in the pan for approximately 5 minutes on each side, until lightly browned.
3. Serve the chicken on top of the lavash.

Sliced Open-Faced London Broil

 Serves 6

 Total Cost: $4.93

Calories per Serving: 338

Fat: 11.9 grams

Protein: 31.4 grams

Sodium: 11.9 grams

Carbohydrates: 26.7 grams

Cholesterol: 43.8 mg

1 pound London broil

¼ cup mustard

Fresh-cracked black pepper, to taste

6 slices hearty grain bread

1 tablespoon extra-virgin olive oil

½ cup brown Demi-Glacé Reduction Sauce (see recipe in Chapter 5)

¼ cup horseradish

Nasturtiums with Mixed Greens (see recipe in Chapter 6) is a wonderful side for the open-faced London broil!

1. Preheat grill or broiler.
2. Rub the steak with mustard and season with pepper. Grill to desired doneness. Let rest for 1 to 2 minutes, then slice thinly on bias.
3. While the steak cooks, toast the bread and brush with oil. Heat the demi-glacé.
4. To serve, layer the meat on the bread with horseradish and drizzle with demi-glacé.

Grilled Vegetable Hero

 Serves 6

 Total Cost: $5.54

 Calories per Serving: 283

Fat: 9.1 grams

Protein: 10.2 grams

Sodium: 388.8 mg

Carbohydrates: 40.8 grams

Cholesterol: 11.1 mg

1 eggplant

1 red pepper

1 Vidalia onion

1 tablespoon extra-virgin olive oil, plus extra for brushing on rolls

6 club rolls

3 ounces goat cheese (optional)

Fresh-cracked black pepper, to taste

1. Preheat oven grill. Slice eggplant, pepper, and onion approximately 1 inch thick; toss in olive oil; place on grill and cook al dente.
2. Split the rolls and brush them with oil. Layer the veggies on the rolls.
3. Sprinkle with cheese and pepper, and serve.

Pita, Please

Pita is a great bread to use for sandwiches. The bread opens up into a pocket, which you can stuff with your favorite goodies. For on-the-go convenience, pita is a pleaser. Try it with any of the sandwich recipes in this chapter.

Calzone

 Serves 6

Total Cost: $2.41

Calories per Serving: 242

Fat: 14.9 grams

Protein: 11.8 grams

Sodium: 638.4 mg

Carbohydrates: 16.3 grams

Cholesterol: 32 mg

3 ounces dried sausage (soppressata)

3 ounces pepperoni

¼ cup fresh oregano, chopped

6 large basil leaves

1 tablespoon olive oil

1 recipe Flatbread dough (see recipe in Chapter 11)

½ cup part-skim ricotta

3 ounces part-skim mozzarella

Kosher salt, to taste

Fresh-cracked black pepper, to taste

1. Preheat oven to 375°F.
2. Finely dice the sausage, pepperoni, oregano, and basil. Brush baking sheet with oil.
3. Roll the dough out to ½-inch thickness and spread with ricotta, mozzarella, sausage, and pepperoni. Sprinkle with the oregano, basil, salt, and pepper.
4. Fold the dough in half and seal the edges. Place on the prepared baking sheet; bake for approximately 30 minutes. Slice into 6 equal portions.

Souvlaki with Raita

 Serves 6

💲 Total Cost: $5.74

Calories per Serving: 322

Fat: 7 grams

Protein: 26.9 grams

Sodium: 360 mg

Carbohydrates: 33.8 grams

Cholesterol: 68.2 mg

1 teaspoon olive oil

1 pound diced boneless lamb (fat removed)

Fresh-cracked black pepper, to taste

¼ cup dry red wine

¼ cup fresh oregano, chopped after measuring

6 pitas

1 cup Raita (see recipe in Chapter 5)

1. Heat the oil in a sauté pan on high heat. Season the lamb with pepper. Sear the lamb quickly, then add the wine. Allow the wine to reduce by half.
2. Remove the pan from the heat and toss in the chopped oregano.
3. Place meat on pitas and serve with Raita.

Fresh Mozzarella and Tomato Salad on Baguette

 Serves 6

 Total Cost: $2.75

Calories per Serving: 357

Fat: 13.5 grams

Protein: 15.2 grams

Sodium: 695.6 mg

Carbohydrates: 44.4 grams

Cholesterol: 20.9 mg

1 baguette (French bread)

6 ounces Fresh Mozzarella
  (see recipe in Chapter 3)

1½ cups Tomato Salad with
  Basil–Pine Nut Dressing
  (see recipe in Chapter 6)

You can put the salad and cheese on the bread and bake it to make pizza.

1. Slice the bread in half lengthwise. Shred the mozzarella on top of the bread slices. Spoon the salad on top.

Cheese Choices

If you are cheese lover, you know that most sandwiches are just not complete without cheese. Feel free to experiment with different cheeses for the sandwiches listed in this chapter. But don't just stick with your favorites. Try a cheese you've never used before; you may just find a new favorite.

Peanut-Coconut Grilled Chicken Sandwich

 Serves 6

  Total Cost: $4.77

Calories per Serving: 505

Fat: 25.3 grams

Protein: 23 grams

Sodium: 639 mg

Carbohydrates: 48.4 grams

Cholesterol: 33.2 mg

¼ cup peanut butter

½ cup coconut milk

¼ cup Chicken Stock (see recipe in Chapter 7)

1 pound boneless, skinless chicken breasts

6 slices whole-grain bread

½ fresh pineapple

Don't confuse coconut milk with the liquid from a fresh coconut. Coconut milk is made with water and coconut meat.

1. Mix together the peanut butter, coconut milk, and stock. Marinate the chicken in this mixture for 4 hours, then remove the chicken and reserve the marinade.
2. Preheat grill.
3. Grill the chicken on each side for approximately 10 minutes.
4. While the chicken is grilling, thoroughly cook the marinade over medium heat in a small saucepan until it is reduced by half.
5. Toast the bread. Slice the chicken on the bias and fan it over the toast. Slice the pineapple and place the slices on top of the chicken. Drizzle reduced marinade over the chicken and pineapple.

Roasted Garlic–Potato Salad Lettuce Rolls

 Serves 6

$ Total Cost: $6.37

Calories per Serving: 275

Fat: 10.7 grams

Protein: 5 grams

Sodium: 73.5 mg

Carbohydrates: 40.6 grams

Cholesterol: 0 mg

6 cooked Idaho potatoes or 12 small cooked red-skinned potatoes

½ bulb roasted garlic (see instructions in Roasted Garlic Served on Crostini recipe in Chapter 3)

1 yellow onion

¼ cup extra-virgin olive oil

2 tablespoons balsamic vinegar

¼ cup fresh parsley, chopped

Fresh-cracked black pepper, to taste

Kosher salt, to taste

1 head large-leaf lettuce

1. Chop the potatoes and mash them with the roasted garlic. Mix potato mixture with all the ingredients except the lettuce. Adjust seasoning to taste. Place the potato salad on lettuce leaves, then roll up.

Nut Butter and Honey on Whole Grain

 Serves 6

Total Cost: $4.35

Calories per Serving: 487

Fat: 25.8 grams

Protein: 17.7 grams

Sodium: 238.7 mg

Carbohydrates: 52 grams

Cholesterol: 0 mg

2 cups nuts (shelled)

12 slices whole-grain bread
   (toast if desired)

6 tablespoons honey

Walnuts and almonds work great in this recipe, although any of your favorite nuts are fine to use.

1. Purée the nuts until a smooth paste forms; spread onto bread and drizzle with honey.

Pear-Filled Calzones

 Serves 10

Total Cost: $4.19
Calories per Serving: 333
Fat: 6.7 grams
Protein: 6.6 grams
Sodium: 39 mg
Carbohydrates: 62.9 grams
Cholesterol: 17 mg

1¼-ounce packet dry active yeast

1 cup plus 2 tablespoons warm water (no hotter than 115°F)

3¾ cups all-purpose flour

Pinch iodized salt

5 ripe pears

1 lemon

¼ cup unsalted butter

2 cups warm milk

¼ cup honey

½ teaspoon ground cloves

½ cup confectioners' sugar

1. In a small bowl, stir the yeast into the warm water. Let stand for 3 to 5 minutes, until foamy. Mix with a few spoonfuls of the flour. Sift together the remaining flour and the salt into a large bowl.
2. Make a "well" in the center of the flour, and pour in the yeast mixture. Gently mix by hand or in a mixer with a dough hook until a soft ball forms. Knead for 5 minutes. Divide the dough into 10 small balls, and place on a floured board. Cover with plastic wrap, and let rest for 1 hour.
3. While the dough rests, peel, core, and slice the pears. Zest and juice the lemon. Cut the butter into 10 portions.
4. Mix together the milk, pears, lemon zest and juice, and honey. Stir in the ground cloves.
5. Preheat oven to 375°F. Roll out the dough balls approximately 1 inch thick on a floured surface. Fill each with the pear mixture, and top with a pat of the butter. Fold over the dough and seal firmly. Let rest on the floured board, covered, for about 1 hour.
6. Lightly grease a baking sheet with the cooking spray. Gently place the calzones on the pan, and bake for 30 to 40 minutes. Remove from oven, place on a plate, and sprinkle with the confectioners' sugar.

CHAPTER 5

SAUCES, DIPS, SPREADS, AND MORE

Fresh Tomato Sauce

 Yields 1 gallon

Total Cost: $1.46

Calories per Serving: 53

Fat: 2.5 grams

Protein: 1.1 grams

Sodium: 6 mg mg

Carbohydrates: 6.1 grams

Cholesterol: 3.9 mg

2 large yellow onions

1 shallot

8 cloves garlic

20 fresh plum tomatoes

10 large fresh basil leaves

3 sprigs fresh oregano leaves

¼ cup fresh parsley

1 tablespoon olive oil

½ cup dry red wine

Fresh-cracked black pepper, to taste

2 tablespoons cold unsalted butter (optional)

1. Dice the onions and mince the shallot and garlic. Chop the tomatoes and herbs.
2. Heat the oil to medium temperature in a large stockpot. Add the onions, shallots, and garlic. Sauté lightly for approximately 2 to 3 minutes, then add the tomatoes. Toss the tomatoes in the onion mixture for approximately 3 minutes. Add the wine and let it reduce for approximately 10 minutes.
3. Add the herbs and pepper. Add the butter, if desired. Adjust seasonings to taste, then remove from heat and serve.

Long-Cooking Traditional Tomato Sauce

 Yields 1 gallon

 Total Cost: $2.70

 Calories per Serving: 58

Fat: 3.4 grams

Protein: 3.1 grams

Sodium: 194.8 mg

Carbohydrates: 3.6 grams

Cholesterol: 7.1 mg

2 large yellow onions

2 shallots

5 cloves garlic

30 fresh plum tomatoes or 4 (28-ounce) cans tomatoes

1 tablespoon olive oil

3 pounds pork bones and/or sausage

1 cup dry red wine

½ gallon water

½ teaspoon dried basil

½ teaspoon dried oregano

½ teaspoon dried parsley

½ teaspoon dried marjoram

Fresh-cracked black peppercorns, to taste

¼–½ teaspoon red pepper flakes (optional)

2 ounces fresh grated Parmesan or Romano cheese

1. Dice the onions, shallots, and garlic. Peel and dice the tomatoes.
2. Heat the oil to medium temperature in a large stockpot. Add the pork bones and/or sausage, onions, shallots, and garlic; lightly brown (approximately 5 to 10 minutes).
3. Add the tomatoes; toss with the pork mixture for approximately 5 minutes.
4. Add the wine, water, herbs, and spices; let simmer for 6 to 8 hours.
5. Adjust seasonings to taste. Remove from heat and serve as desired, topped with cheese.

Demi-Glacé Reduction Sauce

Yields 1 quart

Total Cost: $1.58

Calories per Serving: 6

Fat: 0 grams

Protein: 0.1 grams

Sodium: 7.1 mg

Carbohydrates: 1.2 grams

Cholesterol: 0 mg

1 gallon stock (vegetable, poultry, brown, seafood, etc.; see Chapter 7 for recipes)

1. Place the stock in a large, shallow saucepan; boil on high heat until reduced to a quarter of the original amount.

Walnut-Parsley Pesto

Yields 1 cup

$ Total Cost: $2.72

Calories per Serving: 172

Fat: 17.6 grams

Protein: 2 grams

Sodium: 112.1 mg

Carbohydrates: 3.2 grams

Cholesterol: 0 mg

½ cup walnuts

8 cloves garlic

1 cup fresh parsley, roughly
   chopped after measuring

¼ cup olive oil

Fresh-cracked black pepper,
   to taste

Kosher salt, to taste

1. Chop the walnuts in a food processor or blender. Add the garlic and process to form a paste. Add the parsley; pulse into the walnut mixture.
2. While the blender is running, drizzle in the oil until the mixture is smooth. Add pepper and salt to taste.

A New Twist on an Old Recipe

Most people are familiar with traditional pesto, which is made with basil and pine nuts, but many prefer this variation with parsley and walnuts. A mix of basil, parsley, and even spinach can be used for variety. You can also use a mixture of pine nuts and walnuts.

Almond-Arugula Pesto

 Yields 1 cup

¼ cup almonds

6 cloves garlic

1 cup arugula, roughly
chopped after measuring

⅓ cup olive oil

Salt, to taste

Fresh-cracked black pepper,
to taste

1. Chop the almonds in a food processor or blender. Add the garlic and process to form a paste. Add the arugula; pulse into the almond mixture.
2. While the blender is running, drizzle in the oil until the mixture is smooth. Add salt and pepper to taste.

Basil-Nut Pesto

 Yields 1 cup

$ Total Cost: $3.31

Calories per Serving: 174

Fat: 17.7 grams

Protein: 2.4 grams

Sodium: 46.4 mg

Carbohydrates: 3.2 grams

Cholesterol: 0 mg

½ cup walnuts

8 cloves garlic

¼ cup fresh basil, chopped

¼ cup olive oil

Fresh-cracked black pepper,
   to taste

Kosher salt, to taste

You can also add ¼ cup of grated Parmesan or Romano cheese—mix it in by hand after you have removed the sauce from the processor or blender.

1. Chop the walnuts in a food processor or blender. Add the garlic and process to form a paste. Add the basil; pulse into the walnut mixture.
2. While the blender is running, drizzle in the oil until the mixture is smooth. Add pepper and salt to taste.

Mango Chutney

 Yields 1 pint

3 mangoes

1 red onion

½ cup fresh cilantro

1 teaspoon fresh lime juice

½ teaspoon fresh-grated lime zest

Fresh-cracked black pepper, to taste

1. Peel and dice the mangoes and onion. Chop the cilantro. Mix together all the ingredients in a medium-size bowl and adjust seasonings to taste.

Peeling Tip

To peel a ripe mango, you can place a spoon, bottom side up, under the skin to remove it easily, without damaging the fruit.

Eggplant Pâté

Serves 6

Total Cost: $1.33

Calories per Serving: 42

Fat: 2.3 grams

Protein: 0.9 grams

Sodium: 47.1 mg

Carbohydrates: 5.2 grams

Cholesterol: 0 mg

1 large eggplant
6 cloves garlic
1 tablespoon olive oil
Fresh-cracked black pepper,
  to taste
Kosher salt, to taste

1. Preheat oven to 350°F.
2. Slice the eggplant in half lengthwise. Mince the garlic. Rub the eggplant with the oil and place on a baking sheet. Sprinkle with garlic, pepper, and salt.
3. Place in the oven and roast for 30 to 45 minutes, until the eggplant is thoroughly cooked and soft. Remove from oven and let cool slightly.
4. Scrape the pulp out and place it in a blender; pulse until it is smooth. Serve as a spread on toasted bread or with crackers.

Apple Chutney

 Yields 1 pint

 Total Cost: $1.08

Calories per Serving: 21

Fat: 0 grams

Protein: 0.1 grams

Sodium: 1.7 mg

Carbohydrates: 5.7 grams

Cholesterol: 0 mg

2 cups ice water

1 tablespoon fresh lemon juice

3 Granny Smith apples

1 shallot

3 sprigs fresh mint

1 tablespoon fresh-grated
   lemon zest

¼ cup white raisins

½ teaspoon ground cinnamon

This is a relatively simple dish that can be used as an entrée. Serve with Focaccia (see recipe in Chapter 11) and a vegetable side dish for a perfect meal.

1. Combine the water and lemon juice in a large mixing bowl. Core and dice the unpeeled apples and place them in the lemon water.
2. Thinly slice the shallot and chop the mint.
3. Thoroughly drain the apples, then mix together all the ingredients in a medium-size saucepan.
4. Bring ingredients to a boil, reduce heat, and let simmer covered until apples are tender, about 40 to 50 minutes.
5. Place in bowl and store in refrigerator until ready to serve.

Red Pepper Coulis

 Yields 1 pint

 Total Cost: $5.14

Calories per Serving: 27

Fat: 1.2 grams

Protein: 0.5 grams

Sodium: 23.9 mg

Carbohydrates: 3.3 grams

Cholesterol: 0 mg

6 red peppers

1 tablespoon olive oil

Kosher salt, to taste

Fresh-cracked black pepper,
   to taste

1. Preheat oven to 375°F.
2. Toss the red peppers with the oil in a medium-size bowl.
   Place the peppers on a baking sheet and put in the oven for
   15 to 20 minutes, until the skins begin to blister and the red
   peppers wilt.
3. Remove from oven and immediately place the red peppers in
   a plastic bag; let sit for approximately 5 minutes, then peel off
   the skin from the peppers. Stem, seed, and dice the peppers.
4. Place the red peppers in a blender and purée until smooth.
   Season with salt and black pepper.

Fresh Tomato Salsa

 Yields 1 pint

 Total Cost: $0.78

 Calories per Serving: 7

Fat: 0 grams

Protein: 0.2 grams

Sodium: 7.1 mg

Carbohydrates: 1.7 grams

Cholesterol: 0 mg

1 red onion

3 ripe beefsteak tomatoes

½ cup fresh cilantro

1 teaspoon fresh lime juice

Tabasco sauce, to taste

Fresh-cracked black pepper,
    to taste

1. Dice the onion and tomatoes and chop the cilantro. Mix
   together all the ingredients in a medium-size bowl; adjust
   seasonings to taste.

Fresh Tomatillo Salsa

Yields 1 cup

Total Cost: $1.01

Calories per Serving: 14

Fat: 0.1 grams

Protein: 0.5 grams

Sodium: 31.7 mg

Carbohydrates: 2.4 grams

Cholesterol: 0 mg

1 cup scallions

6 tomatillos

¼ cup fresh cilantro

1 teaspoon olive oil

¼ teaspoon dried red pepper flakes (optional)

Fresh-cracked black pepper, to taste

1. Chop the scallions, tomatillos, and cilantro. Mix together all the ingredients in a medium-size bowl; adjust seasonings to taste.

Compound Butter

 Yields 1 pint

 Total Cost: $0.33

 Calories per Serving: 94

Fat: 10.5 grams

Protein: 0.1 grams

Sodium: 9.7 mg

Carbohydrates: 0.2 grams

Cholesterol: 27.9 mg

1 pound unsalted butter

1 cup fresh parsley, chopped

8 cloves garlic, minced

Fresh-cracked black pepper,
   to taste

Kosher salt, to taste

1. Allow the butter to soften at room temperature.
2. In a medium-size bowl, thoroughly mix together the parsley, garlic, and butter. Season with pepper and salt to taste.
3. Spread onto wax paper or plastic wrap, and wrap tightly. Freeze completely, then slice into small pats.

Uses of Flavored Butters

In addition to serving flavored butter with crusty bread at the table, you can use it in the kitchen while cooking. For example, place a slice on top of the item you are preparing or getting ready to serve and it will melt, imparting its flavor to the dish. Compound butter is also good to serve with light poached dishes.

Raita (Cucumber Sauce)

 Yields 1 pint

Total Cost: $1.38

Calories per Serving: 15

Fat: 0 grams

Protein: 0.7 grams

Sodium: 8.5 mg

Carbohydrates: 7.8 grams

Cholesterol: 0.1 mg

2 European cucumbers

1 large red onion

½ cup plain nonfat yogurt

Fresh-cracked black pepper,
   to taste

1. Peel and small-dice the cucumbers and onion. Mix all the ingredients together, and serve.

Balsamic Reduction

 Yields 1 cup

$ Total Cost: $4.55

Calories per Serving: 29

Fat: 0.6 grams

Protein: 0.1 grams

Sodium: 6 mg

Carbohydrates: 4.6 grams

Cholesterol: 1.6 mg

1 quart balsamic vinegar (or other vinegar)

2 tablespoons cold unsalted butter (optional)

To get the very best flavor, it is worth purchasing a high-quality vinegar instead of going for the cheaper kinds.

1. Heat the vinegar in a large, shallow pan on medium-high. Allow the mixture to boil until reduced to 1 cup. Cut the butter into thin pats and whisk them into the reduced vinegar to aid in thickening.

Basic Velouté

 Yields ½ gallon

 Total Cost: $1.60

 Calories per Serving: 8

Fat: 0.2 grams

Protein: 0.1 grams

Sodium: 7 mg

Carbohydrates: 1.3 grams

Cholesterol: 0 mg

1 tablespoon olive oil

1 tablespoon flour

1 gallon stock (vegetable, poultry, beef, fish, or seafood; see recipes in Chapter 7)

1. Heat the oil slightly on medium heat. Using a wooden spoon, mix in the flour. Whisk in the stock and simmer until reduced by half.
2. Remove from heat and cool in an ice water bath. Place in freezer-safe containers. Store in freezer.

Using Butter
When making velouté you can use butter in place of oil for a richer flavor. However, keep in mind that using butter is not strictly in keeping with a Mediterranean diet.

Vinaigrette

Yields 1½ cups

💲 Total Cost: $0.98

Calories per Serving: 140

Fat: 15 grams

Protein: 0.2 grams

Sodium: 1 mg

Carbohydrates: 0.6 grams

Cholesterol: 0 mg

½ teaspoon fresh ginger

4 cloves garlic

½ cup scallions

⅔ cup extra-virgin olive oil

⅓ cup rice vinegar

1. Mince the ginger and garlic. Trim the scallions and slice thinly. In a medium-size bowl, mix together all the ingredients.

Béchamel

 Yields 1 pint

$ Total Cost: $0.56

Calories per Serving: 25

Fat: 0.5 grams

Protein: 2 grams

Sodium: 23 mg

Carbohydrates: 3 grams

Cholesterol: 1 mg

2 cups skim or soy milk

1 teaspoon extra-virgin
   olive oil

1 teaspoon unbleached flour

Fresh-cracked black pepper,
   to taste

Kosher salt, to taste

1. Heat the milk to near boiling in a small saucepan. While the milk heats, mix together the oil and flour. Whisk the flour mixture (roux) into the heated milk. Season with pepper and salt.

Red Wine Reduction

 Yields 1 cup

Total Cost: $4.69

Calories per Serving: 29

Fat: 3 grams

Protein: 0.1 grams

Sodium: 1 mg

Carbohydrates: 1 grams

Cholesterol: 2 mg

1 quart dry red wine

2 tablespoons cold unsalted
   butter (optional)

1. Heat the wine in a large, shallow pan on medium-high.
   Allow the mixture to boil until reduced to 1 cup. Cut the butter into thin pats and whisk them into the reduced wine to
   aid in thickening.

Seasoned Oil

 Yields 1 pint

Total Cost: $0.55

Calories per Serving: 120

Fat: 13.5 grams

Protein: 0.3 grams

Sodium: 0.3 mg

Carbohydrates: 0.1 grams

Cholesterol: 0 mg

2 cups olive oil

5 cloves garlic (optional)

2 sprigs fresh tarragon

1. Place all the ingredients in a bottle and store for up to 1 month in the refrigerator.

Alert

Exercise extreme caution in storing seasoned oil in the refrigerator. Make sure to discard it after 1 month to avoid botulism.

The $7 a Meal Mediterranean Cookbook

Spicy Mango Sauce

 Yields ½ cup

$ Total Cost: $1.36

Calories per Serving: 36

Fat: 0.1 grams

Protein: 0.2 grams

Sodium: 1.1 mg

Carbohydrates: 9 grams

Cholesterol: 0 mg

¼ Scotch bonnet pepper

1 unripe mango

¼ teaspoon vinegar

¼ teaspoon honey

Salt, to taste

1. Stem, seed, devein, and mince the pepper. Chop the mango. Place all the ingredients in a small saucepan and simmer for 5 minutes on medium heat.

Caution!
Scotch bonnet, serrano, cayenne, and habanero peppers are extremely hot; make sure to wear rubber gloves when handling them.

Greek Rub

 Makes 4 servings

$ Total Cost: $1.03

Calories per Serving: 4

Fat: 0 grams

Protein: 0.2 grams

Sodium: 2.2 mg

Carbohydrates: 0.9 grams

Cholesterol: 0 mg

2 tablespoons fresh parsley, chopped

2 teaspoons fresh oregano, chopped

2 teaspoons fresh rosemary, chopped

1 tablespoon lemon zest

1 teaspoon garlic powder

Freshly cracked black pepper, to taste

1. Combine all the ingredients in a small bowl and mix thoroughly. Can be made the day before and stored refrigerated in an airtight container until ready to use.

Turkish Rub

Makes 4 servings

Total Cost: $2.09

Calories per Serving: 9

Fat: 0.1 grams

Protein: 0.3 grams

Sodium: 1.5 mg

Carbohydrates: 1 grams

Cholesterol: 0 mg

2 tablespoons chopped fresh
  mint

3 cloves garlic, minced

1 tablespoon grated fresh
  ginger

1 teaspoon ground cinnamon

1 teaspoon ground cumin

Fresh-cracked black pepper,
  to taste

1. Combine all the ingredients in a small bowl and mix
   thoroughly.

Sweet-and-Sour Relish

 Yields ½ cup

$ Total Cost: $1.92

Calories per Serving: 24

Fat: 0.2 grams

Protein: 0.7 grams

Sodium: 2.7 mg

Carbohydrates: 5.6 grams

Cholesterol: 0 mg

1 European cucumber

Zest and juice of 1 lime

1 teaspoon honey

1 teaspoon vinegar

1. Peel and dice the cucumber. Mix together all the ingredients, and chill.

Difference in Cucumbers
The main difference between European cucumbers and regular cucumbers is that European cucumbers have no seeds. They also taste a bit sweeter. To substitute regular cucumbers for European, simply remove the seeds.

Quick Aioli

 Serves 6

 Total Cost: $1.07
Calories per Serving: 280
Fat: 31.2 grams
Protein: 0.1 grams
Sodium: 273.7 mg
Carbohydrates: 0.8 grams
Cholesterol: 0 mg

4 cloves garlic
¼ teaspoon salt
1 cup mayonnaise
1 teaspoon lemon juice
1 tablespoon olive oil

1. Mince the garlic, sprinkle it with the salt, and continue mincing. Turn the knife blade parallel to the cutting board and mash the garlic and salt into a paste.
2. Put garlic paste in a bowl with the mayonnaise and whisk together. Add lemon juice and whisk again.
3. Pour oil in a stream while whisking it into the mayonnaise mixture.

Sun-Dried Tomato Vinaigrette

 Serves 8

 Total Cost: $1.14

Calories per Serving: 182.1

Fat: 20 grams

Protein: 0.1 grams

Sodium: 29 mg

Carbohydrates: 0.9 grams

Cholesterol: 0 mg

1 teaspoon minced garlic

3 tablespoons red wine vinegar

1 tablespoon balsamic vinegar

1 cup olive oil

¼ cup minced sun-dried tomatoes

1 tablespoon chopped fresh basil

Salt and pepper to taste

1. Combine garlic and vinegars in a bowl with a whisk.
2. Drizzle in the oil while whisking until all of it has been incorporated.
3. Stir in tomatoes and basil. Season with salt and pepper.

CHAPTER 6
SALADS

Tomato Salad with Basil–Pine Nut Dressing

Serves 6

$ Total Cost: $6.55

Calories per Serving: 194

Fat: 16.8 grams

Protein: 2.8 grams

Sodium: 187.2 mg

Carbohydrates: 10.6 grams

Cholesterol: 0 mg

1 large Vidalia onion

4 large ripe tomatoes

3 tablespoons extra-virgin olive oil

½ cup fresh basil

¼ cup kalamata olives

⅓ cup pine nuts

6 cloves roasted garlic (see instructions in Roasted Garlic Served on Crostini recipe in Chapter 3)

Fresh-cracked black pepper, to taste

1. Thinly slice the onion, and cut the tomatoes into large wedges; combine in a mixing bowl and drizzle with oil. Thinly slice the basil leaves and olives; set aside.
2. Dry-sauté the pine nuts (without oil) over medium heat until light brown, approximately 1 to 2 minutes. Blend the garlic to form a paste, then add the pine nuts, basil leaves, and pepper. (You can use a blender or mortar and pestle.)
3. Dollop the garlic mixture over the tomatoes and onions. Adjust seasonings to taste. To serve, place in a bowl and garnish with the olive slices.

Grapefruit-Pomegranate Salad

 Serves 6

$ Total Cost: $6.26

Calories per Serving: 118

Fat: 4.7 grams

Protein: 2.8 grams

Sodium: 226.9 mg

Carbohydrates: 13.3 grams

Cholesterol: 12.5 mg

2 ruby red grapefruits

3 ounces Parmesan

1 pomegranate

6 cups mesclun leaves

¼ cup Basic Vegetable Stock
(see recipe in Chapter 7)

1. Peel the grapefruit with a knife, completely removing all the pith (the white layer under the skin). Cut out each section with the knife, again ensuring that no pith remains. Shave Parmesan with a vegetable peeler to form curls. Peel the pomegranate carefully with a paring knife; carefully remove berries/seeds.
2. Toss the mesclun greens in the stock.
3. To serve, mound the greens on serving plates and arrange the grapefruit sections, cheese, and pomegranate on top.

What Is the Pith?
The pith is that white layer under the skin of the grapefruit. Its bitter flavor will detract from your dish.

Baby Greens with Emulsion Vinaigrette

 Serves 6

 Total Cost: $5.48

Calories per Serving: 121

Fat: 9.1 grams

Protein: 1.2 grams

Sodium: 43.5 mg

Carbohydrates: 8 grams

Cholesterol: 0 mg

¼ cup cooked chickpeas

2 cloves garlic, minced

½ bulb shallot, minced

¼ cup fresh parsley, chopped

¼ cup extra-virgin olive oil

½ cup balsamic vinegar

Fresh-cracked black pepper, to taste

6 cups baby salad green mix

1. In a blender or food processor, purée the chickpeas. Add the garlic, shallots, and parsley; pulse until well incorporated.
2. Turn on the blender to "mix" setting. Add the oil and vinegar until the mixture emulsifies. Season to taste with pepper.
3. Drizzle vinaigrette over bed of baby salad greens.

Almond and Pear with Gorgonzola

 Serves 6

3 ounces orange juice

3 red pears

6 cups watercress

3 ounces almonds, slivered

3 ounces Gorgonzola

1 tablespoon extra-virgin
olive oil

1. In a large mixing bowl, mix the orange juice with enough ice water to cover the pears. Slice the pears in half, remove the cores, and then slice the pears thinly; add them to the orange juice mixture.
2. Mound the watercress on individual plates or a serving platter.
3. Drain the pears and fan the slices on each plate around the watercress. Sprinkle with the almond slivers. Scatter the crumbled Gorgonzola atop. Drizzle a bit of extra-virgin olive oil over each serving, and serve.

Roasted-Beet Slaw

 Serves 6

 Total Cost: $2.08

Calories per Serving: 97

Fat: 5.3 grams

Protein: 1.3 grams

Sodium: 85.3 mg

Carbohydrates: 11.7 grams

Cholesterol: 0 mg

3 large beets (thoroughly cleaned and unpeeled)

2 tablespoons olive oil

1 teaspoon coarse salt

¼ cup balsamic vinegar

3 cups thinly sliced bitter greens (collard, kale, etc.)

¼ cup raisins

1 teaspoon toasted pine nuts (for dry-sautéting instructions see Tomato Salad with Basil–Pine Nut Dressing recipe in this chapter)

Kosher salt, to taste

Fresh-cracked black pepper, to taste

The unique flavor of fresh beets is quite unlike that of the canned or jarred beets you may have known as a child.

1. Preheat oven to 350°F.
2. Toss the beets in the oil. Sprinkle the teaspoon of coarse salt in a sheet pan and place the beets on salt bed; roast for approximately 1 to 1½ hours, until the beets are fork tender.
3. While the beets are roasting, heat the balsamic vinegar in a large sauté pan. Add the greens and raisins; heat just long enough for the greens to wilt and the raisins to plump a little.
4. Remove the beets from the oven and peel and finely slice them. Mix together the beets, greens, and pine nuts; season with salt and pepper, and serve.

Cooking Beets

Cook beets in their skin to prevent loss of color. This will work for any cooking method.

Fennel Salad with Garlic Oil

 Serves 4

 Total Cost: $6.19

Calories per Serving: 243

Fat: 24.8 grams

Protein: 1.2 grams

Sodium: 35.4 mg

Carbohydrates: 3.1 grams

Cholesterol: 0 mg

½ cup olive oil, divided

2 garlic cloves, peeled and lightly crushed

1 cup sliced fennel bulb

¼ teaspoon kosher salt

Freshly cracked black pepper, to taste

1 teaspoon lemon zest

4 cups baby spinach greens

1. Combine half the olive oil and the garlic in a small nonstick skillet over medium heat. Cook until the garlic begins to sizzle. Remove the garlic with a slotted spoon and discard. Add the fennel and quickly stir-fry to coat with oil and just warm through, about 1 to 2 minutes.
2. Remove the skillet from the heat. Add to the skillet the remaining oil and the salt, pepper, and lemon zest.
3. To serve, equally divide the greens among 4 salad plates. Use a slotted spoon to remove the fennel from the skillet. Equally divide the fennel and place in the center of the greens. Serve the remaining garlic-flavored oil on the side.

Arugula Salad with Summer Squash

 Serves 6

 Total Cost: $5.20

Calories per Serving: 181

Fat: 16 grams

Protein: 6.3 grams

Sodium: 227.7 mg

Carbohydrates: 4.2 grams

Cholesterol: 18.3 mg

¼ cup extra-virgin olive oil

2 tablespoons lemon juice

1 tablespoon minced shallot

¼ teaspoon salt

⅛ teaspoon black pepper, to taste

1 pound green and yellow summer squash, sliced

4 lightly packed cups roughly chopped arugula

¼ packed cup fresh basil leaves, torn into small pieces

5 ounces goat cheese, crumbled

1. Combine the oil, lemon juice, shallot, salt, and pepper in a large nonreactive bowl and whisk to mix. Add the squash, toss to coat, and let stand for 3 minutes. Add the arugula and basil and toss to combine. Arrange the salad on a serving platter or individual chilled plates and sprinkle with the goat cheese. Serve immediately.

Nasturtiums with Mixed Greens

 Serves 6

6 cups baby salad greens

12 nasturtiums

6 ounces red grapes

¼ cup fresh parsley

2 tablespoons extra-virgin olive oil

3 tablespoons fresh orange juice

½ tablespoon fresh lime juice

1 teaspoon capers

Fresh-crushed black pepper, to taste

Nasturtiums tend to have a peppery flavor, so go easy on the added black pepper.

1. Gently clean the greens and nasturtiums in cold water. Cut the grapes in half and chop the parsley.
2. Blend the oil, orange and lime juice, and chopped parsley.
3. Place the greens on plates and top with nasturtiums. Drizzle with oil and citrus mixture. Sprinkle with sliced grapes and capers, and season with pepper.

Edible Flowers

Edible flowers are an incredible way to add a touch of romance to your dishes. Use them often to remind you of the seductive Mediterranean style of living and cooking. Pansies, marigolds, and calendulas are also edible flowers, and remember that all flowers used should be grown without pesticides.

Pasta and Crab Salad

 Serves 6

12 ounces farfalle

6 tablespoons olive oil

3 tablespoons lemon juice

2 cloves garlic, minced

Salt, to taste

Freshly ground pepper, to taste

1 6-ounce can crabmeat

4 scallions, sliced

1 cup radishes, chopped

2 tablespoons fresh parsley, chopped

1. Cook the pasta al dente; drain.
2. Combine the olive oil, lemon juice, garlic, salt, and pepper. Mix together the crab, scallions, radishes, and parsley.
3. Mix the pasta with the olive oil mixture and let stand 5 minutes.
4. Add the crab mixture, toss again, and serve.

Pesto Pasta Salad

 Serves 4

💲 Total Cost: $6.44

📍 Calories per Serving: 478

Fat: 30.2 grams

Protein: 16.9 grams

Sodium: 561.5 mg

Carbohydrates: 36.5 grams

Cholesterol: 21.3 mg

1 cup pesto (see recipes in Chapter 5)

4 cups cooked penne pasta

¼ cup diced red onion

¼ cup sliced black olives

½ cup cherry tomatoes

¼ cup diced roasted red bell peppers (for roasting instructions see Bruschetta with Marinated Red Pepper recipe in Chapter 3)

1 2-ounce can chopped artichoke hearts, drained

4 ounces cubed ham

4 ounces cubed provolone cheese

1 clove minced garlic

1. Combine all ingredients and chill.

Pasta Salad Niçoise

 Serves: 4

$ Total Cost: $5.11

Calories per Serving: 297

Fat: 9.3 grams

Protein: 15.6 grams

Sodium: 311.7 mg

Carbohydrates: 33 grams

Cholesterol: 17.8 mg

¼ cup low-fat Italian dressing

¼ cup chopped fresh basil

2 cloves minced garlic

¼ teaspoon red pepper flakes

2 cups small shell pasta, cooked, drained, and chilled

1 6-ounce can water-packed albacore tuna, drained and flaked

¾ cup diced tomato

½ avocado, peeled and diced

¼ cup thinly sliced red onion

2 tablespoons chopped black olives

4 lettuce leaves

1. In a small bowl, stir together the dressing, basil, garlic, and red pepper flakes. In a large bowl, combine the pasta, tuna, tomato, avocado, red onion, and olives. Add dressing and toss well. Line 4 plates with the lettuce leaves. Spoon the pasta mixture on the lettuce, dividing evenly. Serve at once.

Marinated Artichoke Hearts

 Serves 6

 Total Cost: $7.00

 Calories per Serving: 67

Fat: 2.5 grams

Protein: 1.9 grams

Sodium: 44.9 mg

Carbohydrates: 9.2 grams

Cholesterol: 0 mg

3 whole artichokes

1 ounce lemon juice

2 ounces dry white wine

1½ cups Basic Vegetable Stock (see recipe in Chapter 7)

1 tablespoon extra-virgin olive oil

½ teaspoon dried thyme

1 teaspoon dried oregano

1 teaspoon dried marjoram

1 teaspoon dried basil

Fresh-cracked black pepper, to taste

1. Peel the stems of the artichokes and remove the large leaves (you can reserve the leaves for a future stock).
2. Slice the artichokes in half lengthwise, including the long stems, and then place the artichoke halves in a sauté pan. Pour in the lemon juice, wine, and stock.
3. Bring to boil for 10 minutes or until the artichokes are fork tender. Remove from heat, strain, and then transfer to a bowl.
4. Add the oil, herbs, and pepper. Let cool, cover, and refrigerate until ready to serve.

Wine Choices and Substitutes

Be careful with your choice of wine, as artichokes tend to make a wine taste tinny. You will want to choose something to match the acidity. Or try simply using lemon juice instead.

Goat Cheese with Sweet-and-Spicy Walnuts on Shredded Celery

 Serves 6

$ Total Cost: $5.66

Calories per Serving: 340

Fat: 29.4 grams

Protein: 10.8 grams

Sodium: 182.8 mg

Carbohydrates: 12.5 grams

Cholesterol: 22.3 mg

1 tablespoon olive oil

2 tablespoons honey

¾ cup walnuts, shelled

1 tablespoon chili powder

Fresh-cracked black pepper,
  to taste

½ cup celery, chopped

6 ounces goat cheese

¼ cup fresh lemon juice

1. Preheat oven to 350°F.
2. In a bowl, mix together the oil and honey, then toss in the nuts. Spread the nut mixture on a baking sheet and sprinkle with the chili powder and pepper; roast in oven for 5 to 10 minutes, until coating is solid and crunchy.
3. Cut off the root ends of the celery and shred the celery in a food processor. Toss together all the ingredients. Serve in mounds on serving plates.

Citrus-Steamed Carrots

 Serves 6

Total Cost: $2.78

Calories per Serving: 86

Fat: 2.6 grams

Protein: 1.2 grams

Sodium: 96.6 mg

Carbohydrates: 16 grams

Cholesterol: 0 mg

1 pound carrots

1 cup orange juice

2 tablespoons lemon juice

2 tablespoons lime juice

3 fresh figs

1 tablespoon extra-virgin
olive oil

1 tablespoon capers

1. Peel and julienne the carrots. In a pot, combine the citrus juices; heat on medium-high. Add the carrots, cover, and steam al dente. Remove from heat and let cool.
2. Cut the figs into wedges. Mound the carrots on serving plates and arrange the figs around the carrots. Sprinkle the olive oil and capers on top, and serve.

Shaved Fennel with Orange Sections and Toasted Hazelnuts

 Serves 6

Total Cost: $5.06

Calories per Serving: 155

Fat: 5.3 grams

Protein: 2.9 grams

Sodium: 62.4 mg

Carbohydrates: 27.6 grams

Cholesterol: 0 mg

3 bulbs fennel

6 oranges

1 teaspoon hazelnuts

3 ounces fresh orange juice

2 tablespoons extra-virgin
   olive oil

1 tablespoon fresh orange zest

Tangelos, mandarin, or any easily sectioned citrus will
work wonderfully with this recipe.

1. Finely slice the fennel bulbs. Remove the peel, pith, and
   seeds from the oranges. With a small paring knife, remove
   each section of the oranges.
2. Form a mound of shaved fennel on each serving plate and
   arrange the orange sections on top. Sprinkle with nuts,
   then drizzle with the orange juice and oil. Finish with a
   sprinkle of zest.

Turkey and Cranberry on Butternut Squash

 Serves 6

 Total Cost: $4.61

 Calories per Serving: 142

Fat: 5.5 grams

Protein: 10.4 grams

Sodium: 622.3 mg

Carbohydrates: 13.7 grams

Cholesterol: 24.2 mg

1 butternut squash (a sweet potato can be substituted)

Salt, to taste

2 tablespoons extra-virgin olive oil

Nutmeg, to taste

12 ounces turkey (fresh roasted)

6 ounces cranberries

3 tablespoons orange juice

Fresh-cracked black pepper, to taste

Kosher salt, to taste

1. Preheat oven to 350°F.
2. Peel the butternut squash and cut it in half lengthwise. Remove and rinse the seeds, and place the seeds on a baking sheet; toast for approximately 5 to 10 minutes, until golden. Sprinkle lightly with salt when done.
3. Thinly slice the butternut squash lengthwise. Brush another baking sheet with 1 tablespoon oil and lay out the squash slices; sprinkle with nutmeg. Roast the squash for approximately 20 to 30 minutes, until fork tender.
4. Let squash cool, then place on plates. Arrange the turkey on top and sprinkle cranberries over the turkey. Drizzle with orange juice and remaining oil. Season with pepper and salt to taste.

Canned or Fresh?

If using canned cranberries, drain first. If using fresh cranberries, sprinkle lightly with sugar and steam until they are slightly soft. Sweetened dried cranberries can also be used.

Potato and Chickpea Curry Salad

 Serves 6

 Total Cost: $3.61

Calories per Serving: 175

Fat: 1.8 grams

Protein: 5.1 grams

Sodium: 206.6 mg

Carbohydrates: 36.6 grams

Cholesterol: 0 mg

1 teaspoon olive oil

1 large yellow onion, sliced

8 ounces chickpeas

1½ tablespoons curry powder

5 cloves garlic, minced

1 bay leaf

4 cups Basic Vegetable Stock (see recipe in Chapter 7)

2 baked potatoes, cubed

¼ bunch celery, cut into small dice

1 pint cherry tomatoes, cut into halves

Kosher salt, to taste

Fresh-cracked black pepper, to taste

1. Heat the oil on medium in a stockpot. Sauté the onion, then add the chickpeas, curry powder, garlic, and bay leaf.
2. Add the stock and simmer for 2 hours. Strain, discard the stock, and allow the chickpea mixture to cool.
3. In large bowl, mix together the chickpea mixture, potatoes, celery, and tomatoes. Season with salt and pepper. Serve with your favorite soup or sandwich.

Dry or Canned Chickpeas?

You can use either dry or canned chickpeas. If using dry chickpeas, don't forget to soak them overnight. Or you could use canned chickpeas without having to worry about a loss of flavor.

Apple with Mascarpone

 Serves 6

1 tablespoon lemon juice

3 Granny Smith apples

3 ounces mascarpone cheese

3 ounces nonfat plain yogurt

¼ cup dried currants or golden
  raisins

¼ cup slivered almonds

1. In a bowl, mix the lemon juice with enough ice-cold water to cover the apples. Core and slice the apples, then place them in the lemon water.
2. Using an electric mixer, mix together the mascarpone and yogurt. Place the mixture in a pastry bag with tip, and pipe the mixture onto a serving plate.
3. Strain the apples and fan them along the edge of the plate. Sprinkle with currants and scatter almonds over the top.

Traditional Greek Salad

 Serves 6

 Total Cost: $6.82

Calories per Serving: 189

Fat: 14.7 grams

Protein: 4.8 grams

Sodium: 562.4 mg

Carbohydrates: 9.3 grams

Cholesterol: 17 mg

½ head iceberg lettuce

½ head romaine

1 red onion

1 cucumber

2 tomatoes

¼ cup fresh oregano

¼ cup extra-virgin olive oil

¾ cup red-wine vinegar

Fresh-cracked black pepper, to taste

3 ounces feta cheese

2 ounces pepperoncini

6 anchovy fillets

½ cup cured Greek olives

1. Tear the lettuces into bite-size pieces. Slice the onion and cucumber into bite-size pieces. Quarter the tomatoes. Build the salad by layering the vegetables on a serving platter or in a bowl.
2. To make the dressing, chop the oregano and mix it with the oil, vinegar, and pepper in a bowl.
3. Drizzle the dressing over the salad. Top with crumbled feta, the pepperoncini, anchovies, and olives.

Presenting the Salad

For a stunning presentation, try slicing the onion and cucumber wafer thin and placing the slices on top of the salad before adding the dressing and toppings.

The $7 a Meal Mediterranean Cookbook

Watercress and Goat Cheese Salad

Serves 2

Total Cost: $6.84

Calories per Serving: 231

Fat: 22.2 grams

Protein: 6.5 grams

Sodium: 491.9 mg

Carbohydrates: 1.3 grams

Cholesterol: 22.1 mg

2 tablespoons raspberry vinegar

½ teaspoon Dijon mustard

2 tablespoons extra-virgin olive oil

¼ teaspoon kosher salt

Fresh-cracked black pepper, to taste

1 tablespoon sliced black olives

1 cup watercress leaves, stems removed

2 ounces goat cheese, crumbled

1. In a medium-sized bowl, whisk together the vinegar, mustard, olive oil, salt, and pepper. Add the olives, watercress, and goat cheese; lightly toss to combine. Taste and adjust seasoning as needed.

Warm Mediterranean Cauliflower Salad

 Serves 4

Total Cost: $6.26
Calories per Serving: 154
Fat: 12 grams
Protein: 5.2 grams
Sodium: 562.9 mg
Carbohydrates: 7.9 grams
Cholesterol: 22.6 mg

1 pound cauliflower florets, chopped

1 clove garlic, peeled and minced

⅓ cup Basic Vegetable Stock (see recipe in Chapter 7)

¼ cup pitted kalamata olives

1 tablespoon capers

¼ cup large-diced red bell peppers

½ cup feta crumbles

¼ cup Greek-style salad dressing

Salt, to taste

Fresh-cracked black pepper, to taste

1. Put the cauliflower, garlic, and stock in a medium-sized saucepan, cover, and simmer for about 8 to 10 minutes, until the cauliflower is tender.
2. Drain the cauliflower, discarding the cooking liquid.
3. Transfer the cauliflower to a medium-sized mixing bowl and add the olives, capers, red peppers, and feta. Toss with salad dressing until evenly coated. Season with salt and pepper to taste. Transfer to a serving platter and serve warm.

Wilted Kale Salad with Roasted Shallots

 Serves 10

 Total Cost: $3.08

 Calories per Serving: 108

Fat: 4 grams

Protein: 2.8 grams

Sodium: 32.6 mg

Carbohydrates: 16.9 grams

Cholesterol: 0 mg

3 large bunches kale

10 bulbs shallots

⅓ cup olive oil

2 tablespoons balsamic vinegar

Coarse salt, to taste

Fresh-cracked black pepper, to taste

1. Preheat oven to 375°F. Clean and dry the kale. Peel the shallots and leave whole.
2. Toss the shallots in the oil and place in a roasting pan. Roast in the oven until fork-tender, about 20 minutes. Remove from oven and slice the shallots in half.
3. While shallots roast, quickly wilt the kale in 2 gallons of boiling water for 1 minute. Remove from heat, drain, and set aside to cool.
4. Serve by mounding the cooked kale in the center of a plate or platter. Top with the shallots, drizzle with the vinegar, and sprinkle with salt and pepper.

CHAPTER 7

STOCKS

Basic Vegetable Stock

 Yields 1 gallon

 Total Cost: $1.58

 Calories per Serving: 22

Fat: 0.1 grams

Protein: 0.6 grams

Sodium: 28.4 mg

Carbohydrates: 5.6 grams

Cholesterol: 0 mg

2 pounds yellow onions

1 pound carrots

1 pound celery

1 cup fresh parsley

1½ gallons water

4 sprigs fresh thyme

2 bay leaves (fresh or dried)

10–20 peppercorns

1. Peel and roughly chop the onions and carrots. Roughly chop the celery (stalks only; no leaves) and fresh parsley.
2. Put the vegetables and water in a stockpot over medium heat; bring to a simmer and cook, uncovered, for 1½ hours.
3. Add the parsley, thyme, bay leaves, and peppercorns, and continue to simmer, uncovered, for 45 minutes. Adjust seasonings to taste as necessary.
4. Remove from heat and strain through a fine mesh strainer into a freezer-safe container. Cool by submerging the pot in a bath of ice and water and store in the freezer until ready to use.

Homemade Stocks

Your homemade stocks add a special quality to all the dishes you add them to. Not only will the flavor of homemade stocks be better than that from purchased bases, but you will have added your own personal touch to any meal. Always cook them uncovered, as covering will cause stock to become cloudy.

White Wine Vegetable Stock

 Yields 1 gallon

$ Total Cost: $2.44

Calories per Serving: 31

Fat: 0.3 grams

Protein: 0.8 grams

Sodium: 20.7 mg mg

Carbohydrates: 5.4 grams

Cholesterol: 0 mg

1½ pounds yellow onions

¼ pound shallots

1 leek

½ pound mushrooms

½ pound parsnips

1 pound celery (stalks only; no leaves)

1 cup fresh parsley

1½ teaspoons olive oil

1 cup pinot grigio white wine (or other light white wine)

1½ gallons water

4 sprigs fresh thyme

2 bay leaves (fresh or dried)

10–20 peppercorns

1. Peel and chop all the vegetables. Chop the parsley.
2. Heat the olive oil on medium in a stockpot. Add the onions, shallots, and leeks; sauté for 3 minutes. Add the mushrooms and parsnips; sauté for 2 minutes. Add the celery; sauté an additional 3 minutes.
3. Pour in the wine and reduce until almost completely evaporated. Add the water and bring to a simmer; cook, uncovered, for 1½ hours.
4. Add the parsley, thyme, bay leaves, and peppercorns; continue to simmer uncovered for 45 minutes.
5. Remove from heat and strain. Cool in an ice-water bath, then transfer to freezer-safe containers and store in freezer until ready to use.

To Peel or Not to Peel?

While some people leave the peels on many vegetables to maintain some nutrients, it is important to note a couple of things: Not all vegetables hold the highest concentration of nutrition in the peel. And, when preparing stocks, some peels—i.e., onions, shallots, garlic, carrots—may give the stock a bitter flavor and may make the stock cloudy as well.

Red Wine Vegetable Stock

 Yields 1 gallon

1½ pounds yellow onions

¼ pound shallots

½ pound carrots

4 cloves garlic

1 pound celery

½ pound tomatoes

½ pound portobello mushrooms

1 cup fresh parsley

1½ teaspoons olive oil

1 cup dry red wine

1½ gallons water

4 springs fresh thyme

2 bay leaves (fresh or dried)

10–20 peppercorns

Use a merlot, pinot noir, or your favorite Mediterranean dry red wine. The richer, more full-bodied the wine, the more flavorful the stock.

1. Peel and chop all the vegetables. Chop the parsley.
2. Heat the olive oil on medium in a stockpot. Add the onions and shallots; caramelize until light brown. Add carrots and sauté for 2 minutes. Add the garlic and celery and sauté an additional 2 minutes. Add the tomatoes and mushrooms, and stir for 1 minute.
3. Pour in the wine and reduce until almost completely evaporated. Add the water and bring to simmer; cook, uncovered, for 1½ hours.
4. Add the parsley, thyme, bay leaves, and peppercorns; continue to simmer uncovered for 45 minutes.
5. Remove from heat, strain, and cool in an ice-water bath. Place in freezer-safe containers and store in the freezer until ready to use.

Chicken Stock

 Yields 1 gallon

Total Cost: $2.51

Calories per Serving: 6

Fat: 0 grams

Protein: 0.1 grams

Sodium: 21 mg mg

Carbohydrates: 1.3 grams

Cholesterol: 0 mg

2 pounds yellow onions

1 pound carrots

1 pound celery

1 cup fresh parsley

4 pounds skinless, bone-in
  chicken

1½ gallons water

4 sprigs fresh thyme

2 dried bay leaves

10–20 peppercorns

1. Peel and chop all the vegetables. Chop the parsley.
2. Place the chicken, vegetables, and water in a stockpot over
   medium heat; bring to simmer and cook for 5 hours.
3. Add the parsley, thyme, bay leaves, and peppercorns; continue to simmer uncovered for 45 minutes.
4. Remove from heat, strain, and cool in an ice-water bath.
   Remove all chicken fat that solidifies at the surface before
   using or freezing.

Turkey Stock

Yields 1 gallon

1½ pounds yellow onions

¼ pound shallots

½ pound carrots

4 cloves garlic

1 pound celery

1 cup fresh parsley

4 pounds skinless, bone-in
    turkey

1½ gallons water

4 sprigs fresh thyme

2 dried bay leaves

10–20 peppercorns

1. Peel and chop all the vegetables. Chop the parsley.
2. Place the turkey, all the vegetables, and the water into a large stockpot over medium heat; simmer, uncovered, for 4½ hours.
3. Add the parsley, thyme, bay leaves, and peppercorns; continue to simmer uncovered for 30 minutes.
4. Remove from heat, strain, and cool in an ice-water bath. Remove all the fat that solidifies at the surface before using or freezing.

Rich Poultry Stock

 Yields 1 gallon

 Total Cost: $5.57

 Calories per Serving: 69

Fat: 1.5 grams

Protein: 3.1 grams

Sodium: 40.3 mg

Carbohydrates: 8.6 grams

Cholesterol: 8.9 mg mg

1½ pounds yellow onions

2 leeks

½ pound carrots

1 pound parsnips

4 cloves garlic

1 pound celery

1 cup fresh parsley

1 tablespoon olive oil

6 pounds any poultry (use meat, bones, and skin)

1 cup dry red wine

2 gallons water

6 sprigs fresh thyme

2 dried bay leaves

10–20 peppercorns

1. Peel and chop all the vegetables. Chop the parsley.
2. Heat the olive oil on medium in a stockpot; add the poultry and brown slightly. Remove the poultry and set it aside. Add the vegetables and sauté until brown. Return the poultry to the stockpot.
3. Add the wine and let it reduce by half, then add the water and simmer, uncovered, for 5½ hours.
4. Add the parsley, thyme, bay leaves, and peppercorns; continue to simmer uncovered for 30 minutes.
5. Remove from heat, strain, and cool in an ice-water bath. Refrigerate overnight, then remove all fat that solidifies on surface before using or freezing.

Beef Stock

 Yields 1 gallon

 Total Cost: $3.40

 Calories per Serving: 31

Fat: 1 grams

Protein: 4 grams

Sodium: 25 mg

Carbohydrates: 3 grams

Cholesterol: 0 mg

3 large yellow onions
½ pound carrots
3 stalks celery
1 cup fresh parsley
1 tablespoon olive oil
5 pounds bone-in beef
3 gallons water

4 sprigs fresh thyme
2 dried bay leaves
10–20 peppercorns

1. Preheat oven to 400°F.
2. Peel and roughly chop all the vegetables. Chop the parsley.
3. Place the oil, beef, and all the vegetables in a large roasting pan; brown in the oven for approximately 30 to 45 minutes.
4. Transfer all the meat and vegetables to a large stockpot with the water. Gently scrape the bottom of the roasting pan to pick up all food residue and add it to the stockpot. Simmer over medium heat, uncovered, for 8 to 10 hours.
5. Add the parsley, thyme, bay leaves, and peppercorns; continue to simmer uncovered for 30 minutes.
6. Remove from heat, strain, and cool in an ice-water bath. Refrigerate overnight, then remove all fat that solidifies on surface before using or freezing.

The Fond

The residue left in the bottom of the pan is known as "fond." If you find you cannot release it all, return the pan to the stovetop, add a small amount of water or wine, and whisk to remove; then add it to the stock. The fond has a high concentration of flavor and should not be discarded.

Hearty Red Wine Brown Stock

 Yields 1 gallon

3 large yellow onions

½ pound carrots

3 stalks celery

1 cup chopped tomatoes (fresh or canned)

1 cup fresh parsley

1 tablespoon olive oil

5 pounds bone-in meat

3 gallons water

1 cup dry red wine

4 sprigs fresh thyme

2 dried bay leaves

10–20 peppercorns

1. Preheat oven to 400°F.
2. Peel and roughly chop all the vegetables. Chop the parsley.
3. Place the oil, beef, and all the vegetables in a large roasting pan; brown in the oven for approximately 45 minutes, stirring frequently to prevent burning.
4. Transfer all the meat and vegetables to a large stockpot with the water.
5. Place the roasting pan on the stovetop on medium heat; pour in the wine to deglaze the pan, gently stirring all the residue from the bottom of the pan. Pour this mixture into the stockpot with the meat and vegetables. Simmer, uncovered, for 8 to 12 hours.
6. Add the parsley, thyme, bay leaves, and peppercorns; continue to simmer for 30 minutes.
7. Remove from heat, strain, and cool in an ice-water bath and discard all fat that solidifies on surface before using or freezing.

Take Out the Fat
This recipe is best prepared a day ahead of time so that you can thoroughly chill and remove all fat.

The $7 a Meal Mediterranean Cookbook

Seafood Stock

 Yields 1 gallon

 Total Cost: $3.20

Calories per Serving: 17

Fat: 0 grams

Protein: .2 grams

Sodium: 11.5 mg

Carbohydrates: 2.7 grams

Cholesterol: 0 mg

4 pounds seafood shells (must be saved up over time from crab, lobster, and shrimp dinners)

3 large yellow onions

¼ pound shallots

1 white leek

½ pound parsnips

2 stalks celery

1 cup fresh parsley

1 cup dry white wine

1½ gallons water

4 sprigs fresh thyme

2 dried bay leaves

10–20 peppercorns

1. Thoroughly rinse the seafood shells in ice-cold water. Peel and roughly chop all the vegetables. Chop the parsley.
2. Place the shells, vegetables, wine, and water in a stockpot over medium heat; bring to a simmer and let cook, uncovered, for 2 hours.
3. Add the parsley, thyme, bay leaves, and peppercorns, and continue to simmer uncovered for 30 minutes.
4. Remove from heat, strain, and cool in an ice-water bath. Place in freezer-safe containers and store in the freezer until ready to use.

Wine Choice
Use semidry to dry Mediterranean white wine. If you have a specific recipe in mind that would be complemented by a sweeter flavor, try experimenting with a Sauternes or a late-harvest wine.

Fish Stock

 Yields 1 gallon

💲 Total Cost: $3.19

Calories per Serving: 33

Fat: 0.9 grams

Protein: 4.7 grams

Sodium: 4.5 mg

Carbohydrates: 1 grams

Cholesterol: 0 mg

4 pounds fish bones and heads (can be bought at most supermarkets or saved up from past fish dinners)

2 large yellow onions

2 white leeks

½ pound parsnips

2 celery stalks

1 cup fresh parsley

1 cup dry white wine

1½ gallons water

4 sprigs fresh thyme

2 dried bay leaves

10–20 peppercorns

White or light fish bones and heads are ideal for making a fish stock. Do not use salmon bones, because it is an oily fish.

1. Thoroughly rinse the fish bones and heads in ice-cold water. Peel and roughly chop all the vegetables. Chop the parsley.
2. Place the fish bones and heads, the vegetables, wine, and water in a stockpot over medium heat; bring to simmer and cook, uncovered, for 1 hour.
3. Add the parsley, thyme, bay leaves, and peppercorns and continue to simmer for 30 minutes.
4. Remove from heat, strain, and cool in an ice-water bath. Place in freezer-safe containers and store in the freezer until ready to use.

CHAPTER 8
SOUPS

Basic Chicken Soup

 Serves 6

5–6 pounds chicken (including giblets)

2 medium carrots

2 stalks celery

4 large yellow onions

¼ cup fresh parsley

12 cups water

Fresh-cracked black pepper, to taste

Kosher salt, to taste

1. Clean, trim, and quarter the chicken. Peel and chop all the vegetables. Chop parsley.
2. Place the chicken and giblets in a stockpot, add the water, and bring to a boil. Reduce heat to a simmer and skim off all foam.
3. Add all the remaining ingredients and simmer uncovered for about 3 hours.
4. Use a sieve to remove the chicken and giblets from the stockpot. Remove the chicken from the bones; discard the bones and giblets. Return the meat to the broth, and serve.

Rustic Presentation

For a rustic presentation or for family-style dining, it is okay to leave the bones in the chicken.

Carrot-Thyme Soup

 Serves 6

Total Cost: $5.02

Calories per Serving: 144

Fat: 4.4 grams

Protein: 5 grams

Sodium: 100.6 mg

Carbohydrates: 22 grams

Cholesterol: 10.3 mg

2 pounds carrots

1 large Vidalia onion

4 potatoes

3 cloves garlic

4 sprigs fresh thyme

1 tablespoon olive oil

6 cups Basic Vegetable Stock (see recipe in Chapter 7)

Salt, to taste

Fresh-cracked black pepper, to taste

4 ounces Gruyère cheese (optional)

1. Peel and dice the carrots, onion, and potatoes. Mince the garlic. Remove thyme leaves from sprigs; discard sprigs.
2. Place the carrots, onions, potatoes, and garlic in large stockpot with the oil. Sweat slowly for approximately 10 minutes.
3. Add the stock and bring to a simmer; cook, uncovered, for approximately 1 hour.
4. Let the mixture cool slightly, then purée in a blender until smooth. Return the purée to the stockpot and add the thyme, salt, and pepper; cook, uncovered, over low heat for another 30 minutes. Serve with grated Gruyère cheese.

Sweating Vegetables
The term "to sweat" refers to the cooking process by which the product is cooked slowly until softened but not browned.

Celery Soup

Serves 6

$ Total Cost: $4.70	
Calories per Serving: 105	
Fat: 4.9 grams	
Protein: 1.8 grams	
Sodium: 151.6 mg	
Carbohydrates: 10.7 grams	
Cholesterol: 0 mg	

1 bunch celery

3 cloves garlic

¼ cup fresh parsley (for garnish)

2 tablespoons olive oil

½ cup dry white wine

6 cups Basic Vegetable Stock (see recipe in Chapter 7)

Freshly ground black pepper, to taste

Salt, to taste

1. Peel and finely chop the celery. Mince the garlic and chop the parsley.
2. Sauté the garlic in the oil over low heat until tender. Add the celery and sauté slightly, then add the wine and reduce by half.
3. Pour in the stock and simmer for about 1 hour, until celery is tender. Season to taste with pepper and salt. Serve with chopped parsley as garnish.

Carrot-Lemon Soup

 Serves 6

Total Cost: $3.48

Calories per Serving: 112

Fat: 6.2 grams

Protein: 1.5 grams

Sodium: 100.2 mg

Carbohydrates: 14.9 grams

Cholesterol: 0 mg

2 pounds carrots

2 large yellow onions

2 cloves garlic

1 fresh lemon

3 tablespoons olive oil

6 cups Basic Vegetable Stock
(see recipe in Chapter 7)

1 teaspoon fresh minced
ginger

Salt, to taste

Fresh-cracked black pepper,
to taste

3 fresh scallions

1. Peel and dice the carrots and onions. Mince the garlic.
   Juice, zest, and grate the lemon.
2. Heat the oil to medium in a large stockpot and lightly sauté
   the carrots, onions, and garlic.
3. Add the stock and simmer for approximately 1 hour. Add the
   ginger, lemon juice, and zest. Season with salt and pepper.
4. Chill and serve with finely chopped scallions as garnish.

Cheese Soup

 Serves 6

 Total Cost: $3.40

 Calories per Serving: 175

Fat: 7.2 grams

Protein: 6.4 grams

Sodium: 147.1 mg

Carbohydrates: 14.5 grams

Cholesterol: 19.7 mg

1 large yellow onion

1 shallot

2 cloves garlic

1 teaspoon olive oil

⅓ cup all-purpose flour

1 cup dry white wine

3 cups Chicken Stock (see recipe in Chapter 7)

Fresh-cracked black pepper, to taste

⅛ teaspoon ground red pepper

1 cup grated Cheddar cheese

1. Dice the onion and mince the shallot and garlic.
2. Heat the oil on medium in a stockpot and sauté the onions, shallots, and garlic until light brown.
3. Add the flour and mix thoroughly. Pour in the wine and let it be absorbed by the flour. Whisk in the stock, black pepper, and red pepper. Cook, uncovered, over medium heat for approximately 30 minutes or until thickened.
4. Remove from heat and add ¾ cup of cheese. Stir to incorporate the cheese. Serve topped with the remaining cheese.

Add Some Broccoli

If you wish to add broccoli to this, steam 6 cups of broccoli florets. Purée ¾ of the product. Add the purée to the soup with the cheese. Use the remaining broccoli as a garnish with the extra cheese.

The $7 a Meal Mediterranean Cookbook

Vegetable Consommé

Serves 6

$ Total Cost: $3.01

Calories per Serving: 68

Fat: 0.7 grams

Protein: 3.2 grams

Sodium: 81.8 mg

Carbohydrates: 13.1 grams

Cholesterol: 0 mg

1 yellow onion

1 leek

1 shallot

3 cloves garlic

2 carrots

½ cup mushrooms

2 stalks celery

1 cup green beans

½ cup fresh parsley

6 sprigs thyme

3 egg whites

6 cups White Wine Vegetable Stock (see recipe in Chapter 7)

2 dried bay leaves

Freshly ground black pepper, to taste

Kosher salt, to taste

1. Peel (as necessary) and chop all the vegetables. Chop the parsley and thyme leaves (discard thyme sprigs).
2. Place all the ingredients in a stockpot and bring to simmer over medium heat. Do not boil. Stir with a wooden spoon until raft forms, then allow to simmer 45 minutes to 1 hour.
3. Ladle the soup from the pot into a colander lined with cheesecloth. Discard raft. Serve clear consommé.

The Raft

The egg will cause the vegetables to form an island on top of the soup. This is called the "raft." The raft draws all the impurities out of the soup. Once it forms, let it float by itself to bask in the warmth of your consommé sea.

Roasted Root Vegetable Soup

 Serves 6

2 parsnips

3 carrots

2 large potatoes

3 stalks celery

3 yellow onions

1 tablespoon olive oil

1 fresh rosemary sprig

4 cups Basic Vegetable Stock (see recipe in Chapter 7)

3 sprigs fresh thyme

¼ cup fresh parsley

2 dried bay leaves

Fresh-cracked black pepper, to taste

Kosher salt (optional)

1. Preheat oven to 375°F.
2. Peel (as necessary) and chop all the vegetables into bite-size pieces.
3. Pour the oil into a large roasting pan. Place the vegetables and rosemary sprig in the pan and roast al dente, probably 30–45 minutes. Remove from oven, discard rosemary sprig, and let vegetables cool slightly.
4. In a blender, purée the roasted vegetables thoroughly in small batches. Add vegetable stock to the blender as needed. Pour the mixture and remaining stock into a stockpot and bring to a simmer over medium heat.
5. Chop the thyme leaves (discard sprigs) and the parsley. Add the remaining ingredients to the pot and continue to simmer for 30 minutes to 1 hour. Remove bay leaves before serving.

Stracciatella (Italian Egg Drop Soup)

 Serves 6

$ Total Cost: $5.46

Calories per Serving: 115

Fat: 4.5 grams

Protein: 7.7 grams

Sodium: 200.5 mg

Carbohydrates: 13.1 grams

Cholesterol: 44.8 mg

1 yellow onion

1 shallot

6 cloves garlic

½ cup fresh parsley

3 sprigs thyme

1 tablespoon olive oil

2 quarts Chicken Stock (see recipe in Chapter 7)

1 dried bay leaf

1 pound fresh spinach

2 whole eggs

4 egg whites

Fresh-cracked black pepper, to taste

2 ounces Parmesan cheese

1. Finely chop the onion and shallot. Mince the garlic and chop the parsley and thyme leaves (discard thyme sprigs).
2. Heat the oil to medium-high temperature in a large stockpot; sauté the onion, shallot, and garlic slightly. Add the stock, bay leaf, parsley, and thyme; simmer for 30 to 45 minutes.
3. Remove the bay leaf. Finely slice the spinach and add it to the simmering stock; let wilt. While it is wilting, whisk the whole eggs and egg whites in a small bowl. Add the eggs to the stock, stir, and simmer until the eggs are cooked. Season with pepper to taste and serve with grated Parmesan.

Always Remove Bay Leaves

Bay leaves should be removed before you serve the dish. Bay leaves have sharp edges that can cut the inside of your throat, and they can also cause some intestinal problems. While they are excellent for flavoring, you must be very careful with them.

Wedding Soup

Serves 6

 Total Cost: $6.52

Calories per Serving: 219

Fat: 8.5 grams

Protein: 17.1 grams

Sodium: 348.8 mg

Carbohydrates: 18.4 grams

Cholesterol: 60.2 mg

3 slices Italian bread, toasted

¾ pound lean ground beef

1 egg

1 yellow onion, chopped

3 cloves garlic, minced

¼ cup fresh parsley, chopped

3 sprigs fresh oregano, chopped

2 sprigs fresh basil, chopped

Fresh-cracked black pepper, to taste

4 ounces freshly grated Parmesan cheese

1 cup rough-chopped fresh spinach (stems removed)

2 quarts Chicken Stock (see recipe in Chapter 7)

1. Preheat oven to 375°F.
2. Wet the toasted Italian bread with water, then squeeze out all the liquid.
3. In a large bowl, mix together the bread, beef, egg, onion, garlic, parsley, oregano leaves, basil, pepper, and half of the Parmesan. Form the mixture into 1- to 2-inch balls; place in a baking dish and cook for 20 to 30 minutes. Remove from oven and drain on paper towels.
4. Steam the spinach al dente. In a large stockpot, combine the stock, spinach, and meatballs; simmer for 30 minutes.
5. Ladle the soup into serving bowls and sprinkle with remaining cheese.

The $7 a Meal Mediterranean Cookbook

Toasted Amaranth for Soups

 Serves 6

$ Total Cost: $3.37

Calories per Serving: 144

Fat: 2 grams

Protein: 5.2 grams

Sodium: 34.8 mg

Carbohydrates: 27.3 grams

Cholesterol: 0 mg

1½ cups amaranth

6 cups of any stock or soup (flavor of your choice; see Chapter 7 as well as this chapter for recipes)

1. To toast the amaranth, toss it in a medium-size saucepan over medium-low heat until the grain is lightly aromatic. Add to simmering soup or broth for approximately 15 minutes before serving.

Amaranth

Amaranth is a high-protein grain that is gaining popularity in the United States. Amaranth can be found in most health food stores and can be substituted for other grains as long as you lightly toast it before using it. Toasting amaranth lightly before using it helps to prevent it from becoming "gummy," but you must be very careful not to burn it.

Pumpkin Soup

Serves 6

 Total Cost: $4.06

Calories per Serving: 100

Fat: 4.6 grams

Protein: 1.8 grams

Sodium: 78.8 mg

Carbohydrates: 14.8 grams

Cholesterol: 0 mg

2 cups large-diced fresh pumpkin, seeds reserved separately

3 leeks, sliced

1½ teaspoons minced fresh ginger

1 tablespoon olive oil

½ teaspoon grated fresh lemon zest

1 teaspoon fresh lemon juice

2 quarts Basic Vegetable Stock (see recipe in Chapter 7)

Kosher salt, to taste

Freshly ground black pepper, to taste

1 tablespoon extra-virgin olive oil

1. Preheat oven to 375°F.
2. Clean the pumpkin seeds thoroughly, place them on a baking sheet, and sprinkle with salt. Roast for approximately 5 to 8 minutes, until light golden.
3. Place the diced pumpkin in a baking dish with the leeks, ginger, and olive oil; roast for 45 minutes to 1 hour, until cooked al dente.
4. Transfer the cooked pumpkin mixture to a large stockpot and add the zest, juice, stock, salt, and pepper; let simmer 30 to 45 minutes.
5. To serve, ladle into serving bowls. Drizzle with extra-virgin olive oil and sprinkle with toasted pumpkin seeds.

Zesting

If you don't have a zester, you can still make lemon zest easily. Simply use your cheese grater, but be careful to grate only the rind and not the white pith, which tends to be bitter.

The $7 a Meal Mediterranean Cookbook

Fish Chowder

Serves 10

3 ears fresh corn

1 leek

1 head fresh kale

3 par-baked (cooked halfway) potatoes

1 tablespoon olive oil

1 8-ounce can crushed tomatoes

1 pound any white/light fish boneless fillet

1 teaspoon curry powder

Fresh-cracked black pepper, to taste

½ cup dry white wine

2 quarts Basic Vegetable Stock (see recipe in Chapter 7)

2 anchovy fillets, mashed

½ teaspoon capers

1. Remove the corn kernels from the cob. Slice the leek and kale. Peel and dice the potatoes.
2. In a large stockpot, heat the oil on medium. Add the potatoes, then stir in the corn, tomatoes, leeks, and fish; sauté until the leeks begin to wilt. Add the curry and black pepper, and then wine; reduce the wine by half.
3. Pour in the stock and simmer for 45 minutes.
4. Add the kale and simmer for 5 minutes, then remove from heat. Ladle into serving bowls and sprinkle with anchovy and capers.

Minestrone

Serves 6

Total Cost: $6.89

Calories per Serving: 195

Fat: 10.4 grams

Protein: 10.1 grams

Sodium: 459.8 mg

Carbohydrates: 13 grams

Cholesterol: 20.8 mg

1 pound Italian sweet sausage

1 leek

1 medium yellow onion

1 shallot

4 cloves garlic

½ head cabbage

1 8-ounce can crushed
tomatoes

4 sprigs fresh marjoram

2 sprigs fresh oregano

¼ cup fresh basil

1 teaspoon olive oil

1 cup dry red wine

2 quarts Basic Vegetable Stock
(see recipe in Chapter 7)

1 cup cooked cannellini beans

1 cup pasta, cooked al dente

Fresh-cracked black pepper,
to taste

3 ounces fresh Parmesan,
grated

1. Slice the sausage into ½-inch coins. Thinly slice the leek.
   Slice the onion and shallot. Mince the garlic. Shred the cabbage and chop the herbs.
2. Heat the oil to medium temperature in a large stockpot. Add
   the sausage, leek, onion, shallot, garlic, cabbage, and tomatoes; sauté for 5 to 10 minutes.
3. Add the wine and let reduce by half. Add the stock and
   herbs; simmer for 3½ to 4 hours.
4. Add the beans and pasta, and let cook for 5 to 10 minutes.
5. Serve with pepper and cheese sprinkled over the top.

Cream of Asparagus Soup

Serves 6

Total Cost: $6.34

Calories per Serving: 105

Fat: 4.0 grams

Protein: 3.7 grams

Sodium: 305.9 mg

Carbohydrates: 12.4 grams

Cholesterol: 0.2 mg

2 pounds asparagus

1 leek

1 shallot

¼ cup fresh parsley

3 sprigs thyme

2 tablespoons olive oil

½ cup dry white wine

1 dried bay leaf

2 quarts White Wine Vegetable Stock (see recipe in Chapter 7) or water

3 tablespoons all-purpose flour

½ cup skim milk

Kosher salt, to taste

Fresh-cracked black pepper, to taste

1. Cut the asparagus into bite-size pieces. Chop the leek and shallot. Chop the parsley and thyme leaves (discard thyme sprigs).
2. Heat the oil to medium temperature in a large stockpot. Add the asparagus, leek, and shallot; sauté for approximately 3 minutes.
3. Add the wine and reduce by half. Add the bay leaf, stock, parsley, and thyme; simmer for 2 to 3 hours. At end of cooking time, discard the bay leaf.
4. In a small bowl, whisk the flour into the milk. Slowly stir the flour mixture into the soup until the flour is completely dissolved and the soup thickens.
5. Serve as is or let cool, purée, and then reheat and season with salt and pepper before serving.

Preparing Asparagus

To prepare asparagus, hold each end of the asparagus and gently bend it until it breaks. Discard the woody end.

Gazpacho

Serves 6

2 large Vidalia or other yellow onions

3 medium cucumbers

1 28-ounce can tomatoes

3 cloves garlic

½ chipotle chili pepper (canned in adobo sauce)

½ cup cilantro

Zest and juice of 1 lime

¼ teaspoon Tabasco sauce

Fresh-cracked black pepper, to taste

1½ quarts Basic Vegetable Stock (see recipe in Chapter 7)

1. Peel and chop all the vegetables into equal-size pieces. Mince the garlic. Chop the chili pepper. Reserve some cilantro sprigs for garnish, and chop the rest.
2. In a mixing bowl, mix together all the ingredients except the stock. Purée all but a quarter of this mixture in a blender. (The last quarter is reserved for garnish.)
3. Add the stock to the puréed mixture. Continue to purée until smooth. Adjust seasonings to taste. To serve, ladle into serving bowls. Garnish with reserved vegetable mixture and cilantro sprigs and serve cold.

Onion-Garlic Soup

Serves 6

$ Total Cost: $5.44

Calories per Serving: 139

Fat: 5 grams

Protein: 7.4 grams

Sodium: 293 mg

Carbohydrates: 15.9 grams

Cholesterol: 11 mg

2 yellow onions

1 red onion

1 Vidalia onion

1 leek

1 shallot

½ bulb garlic

1 tablespoon olive oil

2 quarts Red Wine Vegetable Stock (see recipe in Chapter 7)

6 thin slices French bread

6 ounces Parmesan cheese, grated

½ bunch scallions, sliced

1. Slice the onions and leek. Mince the shallot and garlic.
2. Heat the oil to medium temperature in a large stockpot. Add the onions and lightly caramelize them, stirring frequently so as to not burn the mixture. Add the leek, shallot, and garlic; sweat for 3 to 5 minutes, until they are wilted and translucent.
3. Pour in the stock and simmer for 3 hours.
4. While the soup cooks, make cheese croutons by placing the bread on a baking sheet. Top evenly with cheese, and place under broiler until the cheese is melted.
5. When the soup is done, ladle it into serving bowls. Chop the scallions. Top the soup with the cheese croutons and scallions.

Velvety Mushroom Bisque

 Serves 6

2 pounds mushrooms (any variety or a combination)

1 teaspoon olive oil

1 quart Basic Vegetable Stock (see recipe in Chapter 7)

1 quart Béchamel (see recipe in Chapter 5)

¼ cup heavy cream

Fresh-cracked black pepper, to taste

4 sprigs thyme, leaves only

1. Clean the mushrooms and cut off any discolored bottom portions of the stems; slice the mushrooms.
2. Heat the oil to medium temperature in a large stockpot; add the mushrooms and sauté for 2 minutes.
3. Add the stock and Béchamel; mix thoroughly. Bring to a slow simmer, stirring frequently throughout so as not to scorch, and let simmer uncovered for 1½ hours.
4. In a separate sauté pan, heat the cream on medium-high temperature.
5. To serve, ladle the soup into serving bowls. Drizzle with cream and top with pepper and thyme.

Cleaning Mushrooms

Mushrooms should not be washed in water since they absorb liquid like a sponge. To clean, use a soft brush or paper towel and scrub the mushrooms thoroughly.

If using portobello mushrooms, scrape out the black part from underneath the cap and discard.

CHAPTER 9

VEGETABLE SIDE DISHES

Stovetop-Braised Escarole

 Serves 6

$ Total Cost: $4.46

Calories per Serving: 99

Fat: 2.1 grams

Protein: 3.9 grams

Sodium: 27.7 mg

Carbohydrates: 14.6 grams

Cholesterol: 0 mg

3 heads of escarole

2 leeks

8 cloves garlic

1 tablespoon olive oil

1 8-ounce can cannellini beans

½ cup dry white wine

2 cups Chicken Stock (see recipe in Chapter 7)

Fresh-cracked black pepper, to taste

1. Rip the escarole into bite-size pieces. Slice the leeks and mince the garlic.
2. Heat the oil to medium temperature in a large Dutch oven (with a lid). Add the escarole, leeks, and garlic; sauté for 1 minute, then add the beans and wine. Stir for 1 minute.
3. Add the stock, cover, and simmer for approximately 20 minutes.
4. Remove from heat. Season with pepper, and serve.

Dutch Oven

If you don't have a Dutch oven, don't throw out this recipe. Any deep pan with a heavy bottom and tight-fitting lid can be substituted for a Dutch oven.

The $7 a Meal Mediterranean Cookbook

Pan-Fried Green Beans

 Serves 6

 Total Cost: $3.12

Calories per Serving: 104

Fat: 6 grams

Protein: 3.6 grams

Sodium: 50 mg

Carbohydrates: 11.7 grams

Cholesterol: 0 mg

2 pounds fresh green beans

1 tablespoon olive oil

⅓ cup shelled walnuts

½ teaspoon fresh-cracked
black pepper

½ teaspoon chili powder

Coarse sea salt or kosher salt,
to taste

Allowing the pan to come up to temperature before adding the beans enables the outside of the beans to be crispy while keeping the inside crunchy.

1. Toss the green beans in half the oil.
2. Finely chop the walnuts in a food processor or blender. Add the pepper and chili powder, and blend. Toss the oiled beans in the nut mixture to coat.
3. Heat the remaining oil to medium-high temperature in a large sauté pan; quickly brown the beans on all sides. Remove from pan and drain on paper towels, then transfer to a platter.
4. Sprinkle with salt, and serve.

Roasted Peppers

 Serves 6

$ Total Cost: $6.23

Calories per Serving: 76

Fat: 4.7 grams

Protein: 1.3 grams

Sodium: 43.5 mg

Carbohydrates: 7.6 grams

Cholesterol: 0 mg

2 tablespoons olive oil

2 green peppers

2 red peppers

6 cloves garlic, minced

Fresh-cracked black pepper,
    to taste

Kosher salt, to taste

1. Pour the olive oil in a stainless steel bowl. Dip the peppers in the olive oil, then roast or grill them on an open flame (reserve the bowl with the oil in it). Quickly submerge the peppers in ice water. Remove the skins, seeds, and pulp.
2. Julienne the peppers and add them to the bowl with the olive oil, along with the garlic, black pepper, and salt.
3. Let sit at room temperature in serving bowl until ready to serve.

The $7 a Meal Mediterranean Cookbook

Braised Radicchio

Serves 6

$ Total Cost: $3.98

Calories per Serving: 71

Fat: 2.5 grams

Protein: 1.6 grams

Sodium: 33.1 mg

Carbohydrates: 10 grams

Cholesterol: 0 mg

2 heads radicchio

2 leeks

3 cloves garlic

1 tablespoon olive oil

¼ cup dry red wine

1 cup orange juice

1 cup Basic Vegetable Stock (see recipe in Chapter 7)

Fresh-cracked black pepper, to taste

Kosher salt, to taste

1. Preheat oven to 375°F.
2. Cut the radicchio heads in half. Cut the leeks including the tops into ½-inch-wide strips. Mince the garlic.
3. Heat the oil in a heavy-bottomed roasting pan to medium temperature on stovetop. Add the radicchio, leeks, and garlic; toss for about 2 minutes.
4. Add the red wine and reduce by half (approximately 2 minutes). Add the orange juice and stock. Remove from stovetop, cover, and place in oven for 25 to 30 minutes.
5. Remove from oven and arrange in a shallow bowl. Sprinkle with pepper and salt.

Cleaning Leeks

Leeks need to be thoroughly cleaned because they collect plenty of dirt while growing. Cut off the bottom of the root and trim tops according to how much of the green will be used in the recipe. Cut in half lengthwise and submerge in cold water. Rub all the dirt out of each layer and dry on clean towels.

Oven-Steamed Spaghetti Squash

 Serves 6

2 spaghetti squashes

1 cup water

¼ cup olive oil

Fresh-cracked black pepper,
   to taste

1. Preheat oven to 350°F.
2. Cut the squashes in half; remove and discard the seeds. Place the squashes cut-side down in a baking dish and pour in the water. Cover the baking dish with a lid or aluminum foil. Steam in the oven for 45 minutes to 1 hour, until fork tender.
3. Remove from oven and let cool slightly. Scrape out the insides of the squashes, spooning the flesh into a serving bowl. Drizzle with olive oil and sprinkle with pepper. Serve with Almond-Arugula Pesto or Fresh Tomato Sauce (see recipes in Chapter 5) or no sauce at all!

Oven Steaming
Oven steaming is a convenient method of healthy food preparation without the hassle of having to watch over a pot on top of the stove.

The $7 a Meal Mediterranean Cookbook

Minted Peas

 Serves 6

$ Total Cost: $3.30

Calories per Serving: 95

Fat: 0.2 grams

Protein: 6 grams

Sodium: 3.4 mg

Carbohydrates: 17.7 grams

Cholesterol: 0 mg

1½ pounds fresh peas

¼ cup fresh mint

1 gallon water

1. Shuck the peas and chop the mint. Bring the water to a boil. Cook the peas al dente, then drain thoroughly and toss with the mint.

Barbecued Corn on the Cob

 Serves 6

Total Cost: $3.64

Calories per Serving: 61

Fat: 1 grams

Protein: 1.6 grams

Sodium: 200.2 mg

Carbohydrates: 12.6 grams

Cholesterol: 0 mg

3 ears corn in husks

1 medium-size red onion

1 red pepper

1 teaspoon olive oil

1 teaspoon fresh-cracked
   black pepper

1 teaspoon kosher salt

To minimize the fat added to your meal, use a pastry brush to paint on the oil.

1. Cut the silk end of the cobs and pull out all silk, leaving the husks intact. Thoroughly soak the whole ears of corn in water for a minimum of 1 hour.
2. Heat grill to medium temperature.
3. Cut the onion in half. Cut the pepper in half and remove seeds and stem. Brush the pepper and onion with the olive oil.
4. Place the pepper, onion halves, and corn on the grill and cook al dente.
5. Dice the cooked onion and pepper while the corn finishes cooking.
6. Remove the husks from the corn and cut the cobs in half. Arrange the cobs, onion, and pepper on a serving platter and season with pepper and salt.

Broccoli Raab with Bread Crumbs

 Serves 6

 Total Cost: $2.84

Calories per Serving: 207

Fat: 8.9 grams

Protein: 11 grams

Sodium: 372.4 mg

Carbohydrates: 20.3 grams

Cholesterol: 8.3 mg

2 tablespoons olive oil

1½ pounds broccoli raab

1¼ cups bread crumbs

1 teaspoon fresh-cracked
   black pepper

2 ounces Parmesan cheese,
   grated (optional)

Using a baking dish that doubles as a serving dish is best. This leaves the layered look of the finished recipe undisturbed.

1. Preheat oven to 375°F. Grease a 13" x 9" baking dish with ¼ tablespoon of the oil.
2. Prepare a large bowl with ice water. Bring 1 quart of water to a boil in a large stockpot. Blanch the broccoli raab to just under al dente and immediately drain in a colander and quickly submerge in ice-water bath. Drain thoroughly.
3. Mix the remaining oil with the bread crumbs. Place the broccoli raab in a baking dish and crumble the bread crumb mixture over the top. Sprinkle with pepper and cheese.
4. Place the dish in the oven for 5 to 10 minutes to heat through, then serve.

Wilted Spinach

 Serves 6

$ Total Cost: $7.00

Calories per Serving: 92

Fat: 3.5 grams

Protein: 5.8 grams

Sodium: 122.6 mg

Carbohydrates: 12.7 grams

Cholesterol: 0 mg

2 pounds fresh spinach

¼ cup almonds

¼ cup golden raisins

¼ cup Chicken Stock (see
   recipe in Chapter 7)

Fresh-cracked black pepper,
   to taste

1. Tear the spinach into bite-size pieces. Finely chop the almonds in a food processor or with a knife. Cut the raisins into small dice.
2. Heat a large sauté pan to medium-high heat. Pour in the stock and add the spinach and almonds all at once. Toss until the spinach is just wilted. Remove from heat and add the raisins. Season with pepper and serve.

Cleaning Greens

Clean spinach by filling a sink or large bowl with cold water. Toss in the spinach and gently agitate it in the water. Allow any dirt to float to the bottom; the spinach will float to the top. Remove, drain, and allow to dry spread out on a clean cotton cloth or paper towels.

Roasted Peppers with Cilantro

Serves 6

$ Total Cost: $6.48

Calories per Serving: 54

Fat: 2.5 grams

Protein: 1.2 grams

Sodium: 11.9 mg

Carbohydrates: 6.8 grams

Cholesterol: 0 mg

4 red peppers

2 green peppers

1 tablespoon olive oil

1 yellow onion

¼ cup fresh cilantro, chopped

½ teaspoon capers

Fresh-cracked black pepper, to taste

1. Preheat oven to 375°F.
2. Cut the peppers in half and remove the stems and seeds. Toss the peppers in the oil, then place on baking pan, skin side up, and cook for 10 to 15 minutes, until their skin blisters.
3. While the peppers roast, dice the onion and chop the cilantro. After peppers are cooked, immediately place them in a plastic bag, seal tightly, and let stand for at least 5 minutes; then peel off the outer skin from the peppers and slice into ½-inch strips.
4. Mix all the ingredients together and serve.

Peeling Peppers

An alternative method for removing the outer skin from peppers is to roast as directed, then completely submerge them in ice water. Experiment with different pepper varieties, but use caution with chili peppers, especially Scotch bonnets/ habaneros, which are used only as a flavoring and not usually eaten whole.

Sautéed Artichoke Hearts

 Serves 6

$ Total Cost: $5.10

Calories per Serving: 214

Fat: 4.8 grams

Protein: 4.8 grams

Sodium: 24.6 mg

Carbohydrates: 37.8 grams

Cholesterol: 0.4 mg

3 cups fresh artichoke hearts

½ cup all-purpose flour

½ cup skim milk

¼ cup of fresh herbs, such as
marjoram, rosemary, basil,
etc.

2 tablespoons olive oil

1. Cut the artichoke hearts in half; dip in the flour, then in
   the milk, then in the flour again. Season with your choice
   of herbs.
2. Heat the oil to medium temperature; sauté the artichokes
   on all sides until golden brown. Drain on rack covered with
   paper towels, then serve.

Sautéed Assorted Mushrooms

 Serves 6

 Total Cost: $3.34

Calories per Serving: 57

Fat: 2.6 grams

Protein: 3.6 grams

Sodium: 6.7 mg

Carbohydrates: 4.9 grams

Cholesterol: 0 mg

1½ pounds assorted
 mushrooms

1 shallot

4 cloves garlic

1 tablespoon olive oil

¼ cup dry white wine

Fresh-cracked black pepper,
 to taste

1 teaspoon dried tarragon

1. Cut and slice the mushrooms. Finely dice the shallot and the garlic.
2. Heat the oil in a large sauté pan to medium temperature, then add the mushrooms, shallots, and garlic; sauté for approximately 10 minutes.
3. Add the wine to the pan and let reduce by half. Remove from heat, season with pepper, then stir in the tarragon. Let the tarragon soften before serving.

Baked Acorn Squash

Serves 6

 Total Cost: $3.35

 Calories per Serving: 119

Fat: 0.3 grams

Protein: 2.4 grams

Sodium: 51.3 grams

Carbohydrates: 30.6 grams

Cholesterol: 0 mg

3 acorn squashes

1 cup Rich Poultry or Basic
Vegetable Stock (see recipes in Chapter 7)

1 teaspoon curry powder

Fresh-cracked black pepper,
to taste

Kosher salt, to taste

1. Preheat oven to 350°F.
2. Cut the squashes in half and remove seeds. Place the
   squashes in a baking dish cut-side up and pour in the stock.
   Sprinkle with the curry powder, pepper, and salt; bake, covered, for 45 minutes.
3. Uncover, baste with pan juices, and bake uncovered for
   another 15 minutes or until fork tender.

Season the Seeds
To make a great garnish for
this dish, season the squash
seeds with some salt, pepper, and curry powder, then
toast them until golden
brown in the oven at 275°F
or on the stovetop.

Braised Cabbage

 Serves 6

 Total Cost: $2.30

 Calories per Serving: 41

Fat: 1.3 grams

Protein: 1.7 grams

Sodium: 78.6 mg

Carbohydrates: 5.7 grams

Cholesterol: 0 mg

1 large head cabbage

2 large yellow onions

1 teaspoon olive oil

1 quart White Wine Vegetable Stock (see recipe in Chapter 7)

2 tablespoons whole-grain mustard

Fresh-cracked black pepper, to taste

Each variety of cabbage has its own distinctive flavor. For this recipe, you may want to try Savoy cabbage first.

1. Preheat oven to 350°F.
2. Shred the cabbage and cut the onions into wedges.
3. Heat the oil in a deep roasting pan to medium temperature on the stovetop. Add the cabbage and onions; sauté until light golden brown.
4. Add stock, mustard, and pepper; bring to simmer, cover, and place in the oven for 45 to 60 minutes. Adjust seasonings to taste before serving.

Roasted Asparagus

 Serves 6

 Total Cost: $2.75

 Calories per Serving: 59

Fat: 4.8 grams

Protein: 3.4 grams

Sodium: 78.1 mg

Carbohydrates: 2.2 grams

Cholesterol: 0 mg

2 bunches asparagus

1 tablespoon extra-virgin
   olive oil

Kosher salt, to taste (optional)

Fresh-cracked black pepper,
   to taste

1. Preheat grill to medium. Rinse clean the asparagus and break off and discard the tough ends. Toss the asparagus in the oil, then drain on a rack and season with salt and pepper. Grill the asparagus for 1 to 2 minutes on each side (cook to desired doneness). Serve immediately.

Roasted Carrots with Rosemary

Serves 6

Total Cost: $0.94

Calories per Serving: 68

Fat: 2.6 grams

Protein: 1 grams

Sodium: 78.4 mg

Carbohydrates: 1.1 grams

Cholesterol: 0 mg

1½ pounds fresh carrots

3 sprigs fresh rosemary

½ tablespoon olive oil

1. Preheat oven to 350°F.
2. Peel and cut the carrots in half lengthwise, then in half widthwise. Remove the leaves from the rosemary sprigs (discard the sprigs). Toss all the ingredients in a large bowl.
3. Place on racked sheet pan and roast for 30 to 45 minutes, until the carrots are al dente.

Uses of Rosemary

Rosemary has been around since the time of the ancient Greeks and has been used for a number of reasons other than just adding flavor to foods. For instance, it has been used as an herbal remedy for nervous conditions, stomachaches, and even for cases of depression. Dried rosemary may also be used. However, be sure to reduce the quantity to taste.

Fried Cauliflower

 Serves 6

 Total Cost: $5.02

Calories per Serving: 185

Fat: 11.5 grams

Protein: 9.4 grams

Sodium: 178.6 mg

Carbohydrates: 15.2 grams

Cholesterol: 38.8 mg

2 heads cauliflower

½ cup fresh parsley, chopped

1 whole egg

2 egg whites

¼ cup grated Parmesan cheese

¼ cup olive oil

Fresh-cracked black pepper, to taste

Excellent as is, or try serving with a dipping sauce, such as a fresh tomato sauce or even a red pepper coulis (see Chapter 5 for sauce recipes).

1. Cut the cauliflower into bite-size pieces. Chop the parsley.
2. Whisk the whole egg with the egg whites, then add the grated cheese and parsley.
3. Heat the oil to medium-high temperature in a large skillet. While the oil comes to temperature, dip the cauliflower in the egg mixture and drain off excess; place in the hot oil and fry on all sides until light golden brown. Drain on rack covered with paper towels. Season with pepper, and serve.

Grilled Fennel

 Serves 6

Total Cost: $2.08

Calories per Serving: 56

Fat: 2.4 grams

Protein: 1.4 grams

Sodium: 99.3 mg

Carbohydrates: 8.5 grams

Cholesterol: 0 mg

3 large bulbs fennel

1 tablespoon olive oil

Fresh-cracked pepper, to taste

Kosher salt, to taste

1. Remove the tops from the fennel and cut the bulbs into 1½-inch-thick slices from bottom to top (not across the bulb).
2. Heat the grill to medium-high. Dip the fennel in the oil, shake off excess, and season with pepper and salt; place on the grill for 2 minutes, then turn position to create an X-shaped mark from the grill rack. Grill 2 minutes longer, then turn over. Repeat process until fennel is tender, then serve.

Fennel Tops

Don't throw out the tops! Fennel tops can be used in stocks, but don't forget about their distinctive licorice flavor. Take that into consideration when adding them to a stock.

Steamed Broccoli

 Serves 6

3 heads broccoli

2 cups water

1. Peel the stems and stalks of the broccoli with a vegetable peeler. Cut the broccoli heads and stems in half lengthwise.
2. In a steamer pot, heat the water to boiling. Place the broccoli in steamer insert, set it over the pot, and cook al dente. The broccoli is done when it can be pierced with a fork; about 6 to 7 minutes. Drain and serve.

Steamers

While steamer pot/pans are ideal, it isn't essential that you own them. You can use a metal colander or strainer in a pot with a lid for steaming vegetables or even fish. An even better idea is to quickly boil any green vegetables and quickly submerge them in ice water. This helps to retain the "greenness."

Broiled Eggplant

 Serves 6

$ Total Cost: $4.22

🍦 Calories per Serving: 70

Fat: 2.0 grams

Protein: 2.3 grams

Sodium: 33.1 mg

Carbohydrates: 13.2 grams

Cholesterol: 0 mg

4 small eggplants
4 cloves garlic
1 tablespoon olive oil
Fresh-cracked black pepper,
   to taste
Kosher salt, to taste

1. Preheat broiler to medium heat.
2. Slice the eggplants lengthwise into ⅛-inch pieces. Peel and mince the garlic. Toss together the eggplant, garlic, and olive oil and place on broiler pan.
3. Broil at medium shelf setting, turning every 2 minutes until golden brown outside and soft inside. Season with pepper and salt.

Broiler Pans

If you plan to do a lot of broiling, purchasing a broiler pan will be a good investment. Broiler pans work well because the vents and grooves allow the grease to drain off of whatever foods are being cooked.

Scallion Tabbouleh

 Serves: 4

$ Total Cost: $5.30

Calories per Serving: 229

Fat: 7.1 grams

Protein: 4.4 grams

Sodium: 16.2 mg

Carbohydrates: 41.5 grams

Cholesterol: 0 mg

1 cup bulgur wheat

2 cups boiling water

½ cup fresh parsley, chopped

⅔ cup raisins

1 cup chopped scallions

⅓ cup lime juice

2 tablespoons olive oil

Salt and pepper to taste

1. In a medium bowl, mix together the bulgur and boiling water. Allow to stand for up to 1 hour, or until tender. Drain the bulgur in a colander to remove excess moisture, then transfer to a serving bowl. Add the parsley, raisins, and scallions. Toss to mix well. In a small bowl, stir together the lime juice, oil, salt, and pepper. Add to the bulgur mixture, toss well, and serve.

St. Tropez Vegetables

 Serves: 6

 Total Cost: $5.59

 Calories per Serving: 96

Fat: 2.2 grams

Protein: 4.4 grams

Sodium: 15.4 mg

Carbohydrates: 17.3 grams

Cholesterol: 0 mg

2 pounds summer squash, cut into ¼-inch-thick slices

2 pounds tomatoes, cut into wedges

1 onion, very thinly sliced

2 teaspoons dried basil

¼ teaspoon pepper

4 teaspoons minced garlic

3 tablespoons pistachio nuts, chopped

1. Preheat oven to 400°F.
2. Cut six 15-inch squares of parchment paper or foil. Place on a work surface. Divide the squash, tomatoes, and onion evenly among the squares, stacking the ingredients. Sprinkle with the basil, pepper, and garlic. Bring together the opposite sides of the square and fold down tightly. Next, fold the ends under to seal in any juices. Place in a shallow baking pan. Bake until the vegetables are tender, about 40 minutes. To test for doneness, open one packet and check for firmness and temperature. (Be careful of steam.) Sprinkle the vegetables with the pistachios just before serving.

Endive Spears with Herb Cheese

 Serves 6

$ Total Cost: $6.04

Calories per Serving: 125

Fat: 13 grams

Protein: 2 grams

Sodium: 186 mg

Carbohydrates: 2 grams

Cholesterol: 35 mg

12 Belgian endive spears

6 ounces flavored Boursin
cheese

Chopped fresh parsley or
watercress sprigs, for
garnish

1. Fan the endive spears on a serving platter. Spread about
   1 teaspoon (½ ounce) of the Boursin cheese at the base of
   each spear. Garnish with chopped parsley (or watercress
   sprigs) and serve.

CHAPTER 10
LEGUMES

Bean Salad

 Serves 6

 Total Cost: $2.75

Calories per Serving: 132

Fat: 5.5 grams

Protein: 3.0 grams

Sodium: 218.5 mg

Carbohydrates: 17.3 grams

Cholesterol: 0 mg

1 large red onion

3 sprigs marjoram

¼ cup kalamata olives

1 cup green beans

½ cup cooked red kidney beans (canned or fresh)

½ cup cooked chickpeas or cannellini beans (canned or fresh)

2 tablespoons extra-virgin olive oil

½ cup balsamic vinegar

Fresh-cracked black pepper, to taste

1. Thinly slice the onion and chop the marjoram. Roughly chop the olives.
2. In boiling water, cook the green beans al dente, then quickly submerge them in ice-cold water and drain thoroughly.
3. Mix together all the ingredients in a large bowl. Adjust seasonings as desired.

Green Vegetables
To maintain a vibrant color when cooking green vegetables, make sure you do not overcook them. Boil the vegetables al dente and then either serve immediately or quickly submerge them in ice water and drain.

Succotash

 Serves 6

Total Cost: $3.49
Calories per Serving: 111
Fat: 1.3 grams
Protein: 5.0 grams
Sodium: 23.6 mg
Carbohydrates: 21.6 grams
Cholesterol: 0.4 mg

½ pound fresh lima beans
2 ears fresh corn
1 large yellow onion
1 red pepper
1 teaspoon olive oil
Fresh-cracked black pepper,
    to taste

1 tablespoon flour
½ cup skim milk
½ cup Basic Vegetable Stock
    (see recipe in Chapter 7)

If you use dried beans, be sure to soak them overnight and then cook them in water until they are al dente.

1. Cook the beans and corn separately in boiling water until just tender (not quite done). Remove the corn kernels from the cobs. Small-dice the onion and red pepper.
2. In a large saucepan, heat the oil to medium temperature, add the onion, and sauté until light golden in color. Add the red pepper and cook for 1 minute. Season with black pepper.
3. Add the beans and corn, sprinkle with flour, and stir. Whisk in the milk and stock; simmer at low heat for approximately 30 to 45 minutes, until the beans and corn are thoroughly cooked.

Lentil-Stuffed Peppers

 Serves 6

Total Cost: $6.72

Calories per Serving: 180

Fat: 4.8 grams

Protein: 10.2 grams

Sodium: 166.9 mg

Carbohydrates: 25.9 grams

Cholesterol: 10.1 mg

2 medium yellow onions

2 stalks celery

2 carrots

6 sprigs oregano

1 tablespoon olive oil

1 cup Basic Vegetable Stock (see recipe in Chapter 7)

3 cups red lentils

6 bell peppers

3 cups vegetable stock (any type; see Chapter 7 for recipes)

3 ounces feta cheese

Fresh-cracked black pepper, to taste

1. Finely dice the onions and celery. Peel and finely dice the carrots. Reserve the top parts of the oregano sprigs and chop the remaining leaves.
2. Heat the oil to medium temperature in a large saucepot. Add the onions, celery, and carrots; sauté for 5 minutes, then add the Basic Vegetable Stock and the lentils. Simmer for 15 to 20 minutes, until the lentils are fully cooked.
3. Cut off the tops of the peppers, leaving the stems attached, and remove the seeds. Place the peppers in a shallow pot with the 3 cups vegetable stock. Cover and simmer for 10 minutes, then remove from heat.
4. In a bowl, mix together the lentil mixture, the chopped oregano, feta, and black pepper; spoon the mixture into the peppers. Serve the peppers with the stem tops ajar. Garnish with reserved oregano tops.

The $7 a Meal Mediterranean Cookbook

Black Bean Confit

Serves 6

 Total Cost: $3.26

 Calories per Serving: 115

Fat: 3.0 grams

Protein: 4.0 grams

Sodium: 69.2 mg

Carbohydrates: 19.1 grams

Cholesterol: 0 mg

1 cup dried black beans

2 quarts water

1 tablespoon virgin olive oil

2 large yellow onions

¼ bunch celery

¼ bunch carrots

3 cloves garlic

1 sprig thyme, leaves only

2 sprigs oregano

¼ cup fresh parsley

2 dried bay leaves

Fresh-cracked black pepper, to taste

1 cup brown Demi-Glacé Reduction Sauce (see recipe in Chapter 5)

1 quart Red Wine Vegetable Stock (see recipe in Chapter 7)

1. Soak the beans in the water overnight; rinse and drain.
2. Preheat oven to 300°F. Grease a large casserole dish with the oil.
3. Medium-dice the onions and celery. Peel and medium-dice the carrots. Mince the garlic. Chop the thyme, oregano, and parsley.
4. Combine all the ingredients, place them in the prepared dish, and cover tightly; bake for 3 hours or until the beans are tender.

Demi-Glacé

Demi-glacés not only make wonderful sauce accompaniments, but they can also be used to fortify flavor in stocks and other recipe preparations.

Chickpea Stew

Serves 6

Total Cost: $3.24

Calories per Serving: 168

Fat: 7.5 grams

Protein: 4.4 grams

Sodium: 216.9 mg

Carbohydrates: 23.2 grams

Cholesterol: 0 mg

1 cup dried chickpeas

1 large eggplant

Kosher salt

1 medium yellow onion

3 cloves garlic

1 large potato

1 large zucchini

1 8-ounce can crushed tomatoes

1 teaspoon fennel seeds

3 tablespoons olive oil

1 cup Basic Vegetable Stock (see recipe in Chapter 7)

Fresh-cracked black pepper, to taste

You'll need to start this dish 1 day in advance. Serve on a bed of rice or pasta. Also, don't forget to serve bread for dipping!

1. Soak the chickpeas overnight in water; rinse and drain.
2. Cube the eggplant and sprinkle it with salt. Place it in a colander and cover with a paper towel; let sit for about 30 minutes, then rinse and pat dry.
3. Meanwhile, chop the onion and mince the garlic. Cube the potato and zucchini. Crush and chop the fennel seeds.
4. Heat the oil in a sauté pan over medium heat. Add the onion and garlic, and sauté for 2 to 3 minutes or until the onion is translucent. Be sure not to let the garlic brown. Add the eggplant and sauté lightly until it becomes golden.
5. Add the tomatoes, potatoes, zucchini, fennel seeds, chickpeas, and stock. Season with salt and pepper to taste. Bring to a boil, cover, and simmer for 30 minutes or until the chickpeas are tender.

Green Pea Coulis

 Serves 4

Total Cost: $4.35

Calories per Serving: 28

Fat: 0.1 grams

Protein: 1.7 grams

Sodium: 24.9 mg

Carbohydrates: 5.3 grams

Cholesterol: 0 mg

1 pound fresh green peas

¼ cup cilantro

2 tablespoons fresh lime juice

¼ cup apple juice

1 cup water

1. Remove the peas from the pods. Chop the cilantro.
2. Bring 1 gallon of water to a boil in a large pot; cook the peas al dente, quickly submerge them in ice water, and immediately drain.
3. In a blender or food processor, purée the peas and cilantro until smooth. Pour in the juices and water, and continue to blend until sauce is the texture of honey.

Kidney Bean Casserole

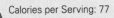 Serves 6

1 teaspoon olive oil

¼ bunch celery

1 yellow onion

½ head romaine lettuce

1 cup puréed carrots

1 cup Basic Vegetable Stock (see recipe in Chapter 7)

1 8-ounce can kidney beans

½ cup cooked barley

3 sprigs thyme, leaves only

½ teaspoon dried oregano leaves

½ teaspoon chili powder

Fresh-cracked black pepper, to taste

1. Preheat oven to 325°F. Grease a casserole or loaf pan with the oil.
2. Slice the celery and onion. Shred the romaine lettuce.
3. Blend together the carrot purée and stock.
4. In the prepared dish, layer the beans, celery, onions, barley, herbs, chili powder, black pepper, and the carrot-stock mixture; cover and bake for 30 to 45 minutes. Serve topped with shredded romaine.

Using Thyme

When using thyme for flavoring, you can use whole clean sprigs and remove them after cooking. If you wish to leave in the thyme, strip the stem of its leaves and add only the leaves to your dish. Or, you could even use thyme as a garnish.

Pasta and Cannellini Beans

 Serves 6

 Total Cost: $3.38

 Calories per Serving: 284

Fat: 2.9 grams

Protein: 10.9 grams

Sodium: 154.2 mg

Carbohydrates: 52.8 grams

Cholesterol: 2.7 mg

1 8-ounce can cannellini beans

1 quart water

6 cloves garlic

1 shallot

2 fresh plum tomatoes

1 teaspoon thyme

1 teaspoon oregano

8 large basil leaves

1 teaspoon olive oil

1 quart Red Wine Vegetable Stock (see recipe in Chapter 7)

1 dried bay leaf

Fresh-cracked black pepper, to taste

1 pound cooked pasta

¼ cup grated Romano cheese

1. Soak the beans overnight in the water; rinse and drain.
2. Mince the garlic and shallot. Chop the tomatoes, thyme, and oregano. Slice the basil.
3. Heat the oil to medium temperature in a large stockpot; quick sauté the garlic and shallots, then add the beans and stock. Simmer on low heat for approximately 3 hours with lid ajar.
4. Add the bay leaf, thyme, and oregano; simmer for 30 minutes more.
5. Add the tomatoes and black pepper; cook for another 30 minutes.
6. Remove from heat, remove the bay leaf, and add the basil. Serve over warm pasta and sprinkle with grated cheese.

Pinto Bean Paste

 Yields 1 pint

 Total Cost: $1.71

 Calories per Serving: 24.6

Fat: 0.2 grams

Protein: 1.2 grams

Sodium: 4.0 mg

Carbohydrates: 4.6 grams

Cholesterol: 0 mg

1 pound dried pinto beans

2 quarts water

2 leeks

4 cloves garlic

2 dried bay leaves

1 sprig thyme, leaves only

2 quarts Basic Vegetable Stock (see recipe in Chapter 7)

1 teaspoon virgin olive oil

Soak the beans a day in advance. You can use Pinto Bean Paste in any Spanish dish. Or try stuffing ravioli with it.

1. Soak the beans overnight in the water; rinse and drain.
2. Thinly slice the leeks and mince the garlic.
3. Place all the ingredients except the oil in a large stockpot and bring to a slow simmer on low heat. Simmer for 3 to 4 hours, until the beans are very tender. Drain and reserve the liquid. Remove the bay leaves.
4. Purée the bean mixture in a blender or food processor until smooth. Add a few spoonfuls of the reserved liquid and the oil to thin the mixture to a paste.

Red Lentil Lasagna

Serves 6

1 tablespoon olive oil

2 cups Béchamel (see recipe in Chapter 5)

1 pound cooked lasagna noodles

½ cup crumbled firm tofu

½ cup cooked red lentils

¼ cup peeled and shredded carrots

1 yellow onion, chopped

4 cloves garlic, minced

½ cup cooked chopped spinach

1 sprig fresh oregano, chopped

1 sprig fresh marjoram, chopped

Fresh-cracked black pepper, to taste

1. Preheat oven to 325°F.
2. Brush a casserole dish with the olive oil. Alternate all the ingredients in the dish in layers, starting with a thin layer of sauce to moisten the bottom before the first layer of noodles, and ending with the Béchamel on top. Cover tightly and bake for 30 to 45 minutes. Cool slightly, cut, and serve.

All about Lentils

Unlike beans, lentils do not need to be presoaked, but they do need to be washed several times in warm water and any debris or small stones will need to be picked out. Lentils are often used as a meat substitute and are a good source of iron. Lentils can be used in salads, in soups, and can be combined with other vegetables and dishes.

Split Pea Pâté

Serves 6

$ Total Cost: $6.88

Calories per Serving: 51

Fat: 0.4 grams

Protein: 7.8 grams

Sodium: 8.4 mg

Carbohydrates: 9.4 grams

Cholesterol: 0 mg

2 cups dried split yellow peas

1 quart water

2 yellow onions

1 sprig fresh thyme, leaves only

¼ cup fresh parsley

2 dried bay leaves

2 quarts Red Wine Vegetable Stock (see recipe in Chapter 7)

4 Roasted Peppers (2 yellow and 2 red only; see recipe in Chapter 9)

½ teaspoon red pepper flakes

1. Soak the peas overnight in the water; rinse and drain.
2. Roughly chop the onions, and chop the thyme and parsley.
3. In a large stockpot, combine the peas, onions, thyme, parsley, bay leaves, and stock; simmer for 3 hours. Drain and let cool. Remove bay leaves.
4. In a blender, purée the pea mixture with 1 red and 1 yellow pepper. Transfer the purée to a large mixing bowl and season with red pepper flakes.
5. Slice the remaining peppers. Fill a loaf pan with half of the purée, place the sliced peppers on top, and finish with the remaining purée. Chill for at least 3 hours.

The $7 a Meal Mediterranean Cookbook

Bean and Lentil Ragout

 Serves 4

$ Total Cost: $3.39

Calories per Serving: 130

Fat: 5.4 grams

Protein: 4.2 grams

Sodium: 96.5 mg

Carbohydrates: 18.8 grams

Cholesterol: 0 mg

1 large yellow onion

1 stalk celery

½ leek

1 carrot

6 fresh tomatoes

3 cloves garlic

2 sprigs thyme, leaves only

¼ cup fresh parsley

2 tablespoons olive oil

½ cup cooked cannellini beans (or 1 6-ounce can)

¼ cup red lentils

¼ cup yellow lentils

2 dried bay leaves

½ teaspoon ground cinnamon

½ teaspoon turmeric or curry powder

½ teaspoon chili powder

½ teaspoon cumin

1 quart Basic Vegetable Stock (see recipe in Chapter 7)

1. Finely dice the onion, celery, and leek. Peel and finely dice the carrot and tomatoes. Mince the garlic and chop the thyme and parsley.
2. Heat the oil in a large stockpot to medium temperature. Add the onions, celery, leeks, carrots, and garlic; sweat for 2 minutes. Add the tomatoes, beans, and lentils; stir for 1 minute. Add the thyme, parsley, bay leaves, and spices; stir for 1 minute, then add the stock. Reduce heat to medium-low, and simmer, uncovered, for 1 hour. Remove bay leaves and adjust seasoning to taste before serving.

Benefits of Beans

Beans are an excellent source of 8 of the 9 essential amino acids needed for building proteins. Essential amino acids cannot be created by the body and therefore can only be obtained through diet. Dried beans also provide you with iron, calcium, and phosphorus. Fresh beans are pretty good sources of vitamins A and C.

Bean Tart with Balsamic Reduction

 Serves 6

  Total Cost: $3.32

Calories per Serving: 238

Fat: 8.4 grams

Protein: 7.9 grams

Sodium: 329.8 mg

Carbohydrates: 32.6 grams

Cholesterol: 13.7 mg

1½ cups steamed sushi rice

3 ounces feta cheese

Fresh-cracked black pepper, to taste

¼ teaspoon Tabasco or other red hot sauce

2 tablespoons olive oil

2 medium yellow onions

3 cloves garlic

1 serrano chili pepper

3 sprigs oregano

½ cup cooked chickpeas (or 1 4-ounce can)

½ cup cooked navy beans

½ cup cooked cannellini beans

½ cup Balsamic Reduction (see recipe in Chapter 5)

1. Preheat oven to 375°F.
2. Prepare the crust by mixing together the rice, feta, pepper, hot sauce, and ½ teaspoon of the oil. Press the mixture into a pie pan and bake for 10 to 15 minutes, until golden brown.
3. Slice the onions and mince the garlic. Mince the serrano. Remove the leaves from the oregano sprigs and chop them. Heat the remaining oil in a sauté pan to medium temperature; sauté the onions, garlic, and serrano. Remove from heat and add the chickpeas, beans, and oregano.
4. Spoon the mixture into the crust; cover with foil and bake for 10 minutes. Cool slightly and serve with Balsamic Reduction sauce.

The $7 a Meal Mediterranean Cookbook

Bean and Nut Patties

 Serves 6

Total Cost: $2.05

Calories per Serving: 172

Fat: 11.3 grams

Protein: 8.7 grams

Sodium: 153.5 mg

Carbohydrates: 10.2 grams

Cholesterol: 42.1 mg

½ cup nuts

1 8-ounce can black beans

1 shallot

8 cloves garlic

2 ounces Parmesan cheese

1 egg

¼ cup Basic Vegetable Stock (see recipe in Chapter 7)

1 teaspoon dried oregano

Fresh-cracked black pepper, to taste

2 teaspoons olive oil

Nuts can be ground in a food processor, spice grinder, or even a coffee grinder.

1. Preheat oven broiler.
2. Grind the nuts. Purée the beans in a blender. Finely dice the shallot and mince the garlic. Grate the cheese. Beat the egg.
3. Combine all the ingredients. Form the mixture into patties and cook under the broiler for 4 minutes on each side.

Allergies Alert

Many people have allergies to nuts or garlic, which are common ingredients in Mediterranean cooking. If you will be serving guests, be sure to find out ahead of time whether any allergies exist.

Chickpea Puffs

 Serves 6

1 2-ounce can chickpeas

¼ cup plain nonfat yogurt

¼ cup soy milk

¼ cup water

¼–½ cup olive oil

½ cup all-purpose unbleached flour

¼ cup spelt flour

¼ teaspoon baking powder

¼ teaspoon iodized salt

½ serrano chili pepper

The serrano chili pepper can be omitted, or you could substitute other chili peppers.

1. Purée the chickpeas in a blender, then add the yogurt, soy milk, water, and 2 tablespoons of the oil; blend thoroughly. Sift together the flours, baking powder, and salt. Combine the wet and dry ingredients. Stem, seed, and chop the serrano; fold it into the mixture. Let the dough rest for 1 hour.

2. Using flour to prevent sticking, form the dough into 1-inch balls. Heat remaining oil to medium-high temperature in a medium-size saucepot. Fry each dough ball until light golden brown and puffed. Drain thoroughly on rack covered with paper towels.

Resting Dough

It is important to allow the dough to rest so that the gluten does not overdevelop. If you try to skip that step, the dough will be much more difficult to deal with and often the end product will be inferior and tough in texture.

Dal

 Serves 6

$ Total Cost: $0.60
Calories per Serving: 65
Fat: 2.4 grams
Protein: 3.2 grams
Sodium: 4.7 mg
Carbohydrates: 8.2 grams
Cholesterol: 0 mg

6 cloves garlic

¼ Scotch bonnet chili pepper

1 tablespoon olive oil

1 cup dried yellow split peas

¾ cup Basic Vegetable Stock
   (see recipe in Chapter 7)

1. Mince the garlic. Stem, seed, and mince the chili pepper.
2. Heat the oil to medium temperature in a medium-size sauce-pot; sauté the garlic and chili for 1 minute.
3. Add the peas and stock; simmer for 1 to 2 hours, until the peas are thoroughly cooked. Serve with Flatbread (see recipe in Chapter 11).

Kidney Bean and Cheese Crackers

 Serves 6

 Total Cost: $1.56

 Calories per Serving: 131

Fat: 6.8 grams

Protein: 6.9 grams

Sodium: 257.3 mg

Carbohydrates: 10.4 grams

Cholesterol: 33.6 mg

1 8-ounce can kidney beans

3 ounces Manchego cheese, grated (Parmesan or Romano can be substituted)

1 egg

2 tablespoons olive oil

½ teaspoon Tabasco or other red hot sauce

½ cup all-purpose white flour

Kosher salt, to taste

1. Preheat oven to 400°F.
2. Purée the beans in a blender. Pulse the grated cheese into the purée, then pulse in the egg and oil. Transfer the mixture to a bowl and stir in the hot sauce and flour.
3. Spread the mixture onto an ungreased baking sheet using a palette knife or spatula, and sprinkle with salt. Bake for approximately 7 to 12 minutes or until lightly golden in color and crisp.

Lentil and Walnut Chili

 Serves 6

$ Total Cost: $3.94

Calories per Serving: 245

Fat: 11.5 grams

Protein: 8.2 grams

Sodium: 49.5 mg

Carbohydrates: 27.7 grams

Cholesterol: 3.6 mg

2 cups red lentils

½ cup walnuts

2 shallots

4 cloves garlic

2 poblano peppers

1 tablespoon olive oil

1½ cups Basic Vegetable Stock (Chapter 7)

2½ cups Fresh Tomato Sauce (see recipe in Chapter 5)

1 teaspoon cumin

1½ tablespoons chili powder

1 tablespoon honey

½ cup plain nonfat yogurt (optional)

If you purchase already-shelled walnuts, be sure to spread them out on a flat surface and search for leftover shell fragments before using them.

1. Wash lentils several times in warm water. Lay them out on a baking sheet and pick out any stones or debris. Chop the walnuts and slice the shallots. Mince the garlic and dice the peppers.
2. Heat the oil to medium temperature in a saucepot. Add the shallots, garlic, and peppers; sauté for 1 to 2 minutes. Add all the remaining ingredients except the lentils and yogurt. Simmer for 1 hour, then add the lentils and cook for 30 minutes longer.
3. Ladle into bowls. Serve with a dollop of yogurt.

Luncheon Egg Encased in Cannellini Beans

 Serves 6

$ Total Cost: $2.18

Calories per Serving: 188

Fat: 12.1 grams

Protein: 8.4 grams

Sodium: 184 mg

Carbohydrates: 11.3 grams

Cholesterol: 199.8 mg

3 tablespoons olive oil

1 8-ounce can beans

½ cup mashed potato

½ cup chives, chopped

2 tablespoons all-purpose flour

¼ teaspoon Tabasco or other red hot sauce

½ cup Basic Vegetable Stock (see recipe in Chapter 7)

6 hard-boiled eggs

1. Preheat oven to 375°F. Grease the bottom of a baking pan with some of the oil.
2. Purée the beans, then combine with potato. Mix the chives, flour, hot sauce, 1 tablespoon of the oil, and the stock with the bean mixture.
3. Mold the bean mixture around the eggs. Place the encased eggs in the prepared baking pan. Drizzle (or spray) the tops and sides of the eggs with the remaining oil; roast for 15 to 20 minutes, until crispy and golden brown.
4. Remove from oven and serve with your favorite sauce (see Chapter 5 for sauce recipes).

Soaking Beans

Dried beans, when submerged for several hours or overnight, absorb much water and swell to as much as twice their original size. They'll cook much more quickly than starting from dried, and the results may be more even, especially if the beans are old. Never cook them in the soaking water.

The $7 a Meal Mediterranean Cookbook

Spicy Roasted Garbanzos

 Serves 8

 Total Cost: $0.82

Calories per Serving: 103

Fat: 4.1 grams

Protein: 3 grams

Sodium: 180.2 mg

Carbohydrates: 13.7 grams

Cholesterol: 0 mg

2 tablespoons olive oil

½ teaspoon each: ground coriander, ground cumin, and red pepper flakes

¼ teaspoon seasoned salt

1 16-ounces can garbanzo beans (chickpeas), rinsed and drained

1. Preheat oven to 400°F. Spray a nonstick baking sheet with nonstick cooking spray and set aside.
2. Combine the oil and seasonings together in a medium-sized bowl. Add the garbanzo beans and toss until evenly coated. Spread out the beans in a single layer on the prepared baking sheet and place in the oven. Shake the pan every 10 minutes to make sure the beans are cooking evenly. Bake for 20 to 30 minutes, until crisp and golden. Let cool slightly before serving. Can be made the day before and kept in an airtight container.

Mediterranean Green Beans

 Serves 4

 Total Cost: $3.28

Calories per Serving: 65.8

Fat: 3.5 grams

Protein: 2 grams

Sodium: 151.5 mg

Carbohydrates: 8.2 grams

Cholesterol: 0 mg

1 pound fresh green beans, ends trimmed, cut into 1-inch pieces

2 teaspoons minced fresh rosemary

1 teaspoon lemon zest

1 tablespoon olive oil

1 tablespoon plus ½ teaspoon kosher salt

Fresh-cracked black pepper, to taste

1. Fill a medium-sized saucepan with cold salted water and bring to a boil over high heat. Add the beans and cook until they are a vibrant green, just about 4 minutes.
2. Drain the beans and transfer to a large bowl. Add the remaining ingredients and toss to coat evenly. Serve warm or at room temperature.

CHAPTER 11

GRAINS

Barley Vegetable Casserole

 Serves 6

$ Total Cost: $2.38

Calories per Serving: 93.2

Fat: 2.6 grams

Protein: 1.7 grams

Sodium: 41.6 mg

Carbohydrates: 16.9 grams

Cholesterol: 0 mg

1 large yellow onion

1 leek

1 carrot

1 beet

1 parsnip

¼ cup cilantro

1 tablespoon olive oil

1 cup barley

½ teaspoon ground cumin

1 quart Basic Vegetable Stock (see recipe in Chapter 7)

Fresh-cracked black pepper, to taste

1. Preheat oven to 350°F.
2. Slice the onion and leek. Peel and finely dice the carrot, beet, and parsnip. Chop the cilantro.
3. Combine all the ingredients in a large casserole dish greased with oil. Cover tightly and bake for 60 minutes.

Casseroles on Cool Evenings
Casseroles are perfect for cool evenings. The oven warms the kitchen, offering a cozy atmosphere in which to work. Once the casserole is in the oven, the cook is free to do other chores while it bakes.

The $7 a Meal Mediterranean Cookbook

Cornmeal Dumplings

 Serves 6

 Total Cost: $0.99

Calories per Serving: 132

Fat: 2.1 grams

Protein: 4.9 grams

Sodium: 61.6 mg

Carbohydrates: 23.8 grams

Cholesterol: 0.4 mg

½ cup cornmeal

½ cup whole-wheat flour

½ teaspoon curry powder

Pinch of iodized salt

1 egg white

¼ cup nonfat yogurt

¼ cup skim milk

1 teaspoon extra-virgin olive oil

1 jalapeño or serrano chili pepper

¼ cup cooked corn

1. Sift together the cornmeal, flour, curry powder, and salt. In a separate bowl, mix together the egg white, yogurt, milk, and oil. Combine the wet and dry ingredients.
2. Stem, seed, and mince the chili pepper; fold it into the dumpling mixture along with the corn.
3. Bring 1½ gallons of water to a boil. Drop dumplings by the teaspoonful into the water (use a spoon to scoop the dumpling mix from the bowl and another spoon to push the dumpling into the boiling water). Cook for approximately 12 to 15 minutes or until the dumplings are cooked through.

Lima Beans and Moroccan Couscous Chili

 Serves 6

1 cup dried lima beans

1 quart water

2 medium yellow onions

1 carrot

1 jalapeño or serrano chili pepper

3 cloves garlic

8 plum tomatoes

1 tablespoon olive oil

1 quart plus 1 cup Chicken Stock (Chapter 7)

1 cup brewed strong coffee (decaf or regular)

½ teaspoon red pepper flakes

1 tablespoon chili powder

1 teaspoon curry powder

Fresh-cracked black pepper, to taste

1 teaspoon honey

1 cup couscous

¼ cup cilantro

1. Soak the beans in the water overnight; rinse and drain.
2. Dice the onions. Peel and grate the carrot. Mince the chili pepper and garlic. Roughly chop the tomatoes.
3. Heat the oil to medium temperature in a large stockpot. Add the onions, carrots, chili pepper, and garlic; sauté for 5 minutes. Reduce heat to low and add the beans, 1 quart chicken stock, coffee, tomatoes, red pepper flakes, chili and curry powders, black pepper, and honey; simmer slowly uncovered for 4 hours.
4. Fifteen minutes before the chili is done, cook the couscous by bringing the remaining cup of chicken stock to a boil. Add the couscous and cook for 2 to 3 minutes. Cover, let sit for 1 minute, then fluff. Keep warm.
5. Adjust seasonings to taste. Chop the cilantro. Ladle the chili into serving bowls, top with the couscous, and sprinkle with the cilantro.

Turning Vegetarian

Almost all recipes that call for a meat or poultry stock can be transformed into a vegetarian meal. Simply substitute a vegetarian stock for the meat or poultry stock and enhance the seasonings!

Rye Dumplings

 Serves 6

Total Cost: $2.75
Calories per Serving: 220
Fat: 18.2 grams
Protein: 2.9 grams
Sodium: 159.8 mg
Carbohydrates: 11.6 grams
Cholesterol: 0 mg

¼ cup rye flour

½ cup all-purpose unbleached
flour

¼ teaspoon salt

½ teaspoon baking soda

2 egg whites

¼ cup soy milk

½ cup olive oil

1. Sift together the flours, salt, and baking soda. Mix together the egg whites, soy milk, and oil.
2. Combine the wet and dry ingredients.
3. Dollop spoonfuls of the mixture into boiling water (or a prepared soup or stew). Cover and simmer for approximately 5 minutes.

Fry Bread

Serves 6

Total Cost: $1.28

Calories per Serving: 222

Fat: 16.6 grams

Protein: 2.3 grams

Sodium: 87.6 mg

Carbohydrates: 16.4 grams

Cholesterol: 0 mg

½ cup all-purpose unbleached
   flour

¼ cup wheat flour

¼ cup cornmeal

¼ teaspoon salt

⅓ cup water

½ cup olive oil

1. Sift together the flours, cornmeal, and salt. Using a dough
   hook or your hands, combine the flour mixture with the
   water and 2 tablespoons of the oil.
2. On a lightly floured surface, roll out the dough ⅛-inch thick
   and cut into desired shapes.
3. Heat the remainder of the oil in a heavy-bottomed skillet
   (preferably cast iron) to medium-high temperature. Fry the
   dough until light golden brown, then drain each on a rack
   covered with paper towels.

Flatbread

Serves 6

Total Cost: $0.82

Calories per Serving: 105

Fat: 4.7 grams

Protein: 2.2 grams

Sodium: 128.6 mg

Carbohydrates: 13.6 grams

Cholesterol: 0 mg

¼ cup spelt flour

¼ cup wheat flour

½ cup all-purpose unbleached
  flour

¼ teaspoon salt

¼ cup water

2 tablespoons olive oil, divided

1. Sift together the flours and salt. Using a dough hook or your hands, combine the flour mixture with the water and 1 tablespoon of the oil.
2. On a floured surface, roll out the dough ⅛-inch thick and cut into desired shapes.
3. Heat the remaining oil in a heavy-bottomed skillet (preferably cast iron) to medium-high temperature and cook the flatbread on each side for 1 to 2 minutes.

Quinoa and Vegetables

 Serves 6

Total Cost: $3.55

Calories per Serving: 100

Fat: 3.2 grams

Protein: 2.9 grams

Sodium: 29.1 mg

Carbohydrates: 15.7 grams

Cholesterol: 0 mg

1 small yellow squash

1 small zucchini squash

1 small eggplant

4 cloves garlic

1 sprig tarragon

1 teaspoon capers

1 tablespoon olive oil

¾ cup quinoa

2½ cups Basic Vegetable Stock (see recipe in Chapter 7)

Fresh-cracked black pepper, to taste

1. Small-dice the squashes and eggplant. Mince the garlic and slice the tarragon leaves (discard stem). Smash the capers.
2. Heat the oil to medium temperature in a medium-size saucepan, then add the vegetables and garlic; sauté for 3 minutes. Add the quinoa, and stir for 1 minute.
3. Add the stock and simmer for approximately 30 minutes with lid slightly ajar, until the quinoa is thoroughly cooked. Remove from heat and add the tarragon, black pepper, and capers.

Quinoa

Quinoa is a grain that is popular in Mediterranean and South American cooking. It is loaded with protein and vital nutrients, and contains all 9 essential amino acids.

The $7 a Meal Mediterranean Cookbook

Pasta and Spinach Casserole

 Serves 6

$ Total Cost: $6.20	
Calories per Serving: 305	
Fat: 12.2 grams	
Protein: 14.1 grams	
Sodium: 202.3 mg	
Carbohydrates: 34.8 grams	
Cholesterol: 14.3 mg	

3 heads fresh spinach

1 shallot

3 cloves garlic

3 ounces goat cheese

3 ounces firm tofu

2 tablespoons olive oil, plus extra for greasing

2½ tablespoons all-purpose unbleached flour

2 cups skim milk

3 cups cooked pasta

¼ cup chopped Spanish olives

Fresh-cracked black pepper, to taste

1. Preheat oven to 350°F.
2. Steam the spinach. Mince the shallot and garlic. Crumble the goat cheese and cut the tofu into small cubes.
3. Heat the 2 tablespoons oil to medium temperature in a medium-size saucepan, then add the flour to form a roux. Whisk in the milk, and cook until thickened to make white sauce.
4. Grease a casserole pan and ladle in the white sauce. Layer the pasta, spinach, cheese, tofu, olives, shallots, garlic, pepper, and more white sauce (in that order). Continue to layer until all ingredients are used. The white sauce should be the top layer.
5. Bake, covered, for approximately 15 to 20 minutes until heated through. Uncover and brown for 5 to 10 minutes longer.

Kale Stuffed with Basmati Rice

 Serves 6

Total Cost: $4.66

Calories per Serving: 238

Fat: 3.8 grams

Protein: 5.0 grams

Sodium: 30.4 mg

Carbohydrates: 45.9 grams

Cholesterol: 0 mg

1 head kale

1 red pepper

1 leek

1 tablespoon olive oil

1½ cups basmati rice

¼ cup sunflower seeds

3 cups stock (flavor of your
choice; see Chapter 7
for recipes)

3 sprigs thyme, leaves only

¼ teaspoon ground cardamom
seeds

½ teaspoon ground cumin

Fresh-cracked black pepper,
to taste

1. Steam the kale. Finely dice the red pepper. Thinly slice the
   whole leek.
2. Heat the oil in a large saucepan and sauté the peppers and
   leeks for approximately 1 minute. Add the rice and seeds;
   toss for 1 minute. Add the stock, thyme, spices, and black
   pepper; cover and simmer for 10 to 15 minutes, until the rice
   is cooked.
3. Lay out the kale leaves, spoon on the rice mixture, and
   fold into rolls. Serve either at room temperature or heated
   slightly in a 375°F oven.

Steamed Teff

 Serves 6

Total Cost: $1.75

Calories per Serving: 183

Fat: 1.1 grams

Protein: 6.5 grams

Sodium: 12.8 mg

Carbohydrates: 36.5 grams

Cholesterol: 0 mg

1½ cups teff

1½ cups stock (flavor of your choice; see Chapter 7 for recipes)

Teff has a mild, nutty, and slightly sweet taste. It is a versatile grain that can be ground into flour, used as a thickener for soups, gravies, and puddings, or in stir-fry, casseroles, salads, and on sandwiches.

1. Combine both ingredients in a small saucepan. Place on stovetop over low heat and simmer for 1 to 1¼ hours.

Spelt Naan

Serves 6

$ Total Cost: $0.66

Calories per Serving: 71.2

Fat: 0.9 grams

Protein: 2.2 grams

Sodium: 1.0 mg

Carbohydrates: 13.7 grams

Cholesterol: 0 mg

¼ cup whole wheat flour

½ cup all-purpose unbleached
   flour

¼ cup water

1 teaspoon olive oil

1. Sift together the flours, then add the water and mix all
   at once; let the dough rest in a warm place for at least
   30 minutes.
2. Knead the dough on a slightly floured board. Roll into 8-inch
   circle.
3. Coat the bottom of a heavy-bottomed fry pan (preferably
   cast iron) with oil and heat to medium temperature; cook
   the naan until golden brown, then cook the other side until
   golden brown.

Spelt and Naan

Spelt flour is a hearty grain
that is high in nutrients. Naan
is an Indian bread that can be
used easily in place of any
type of bread. Chickpea flour
may be substituted for spelt
flour if that is what you have
on hand or simply prefer.

Spinach Barley Gnocchi

 Serves 6

 Total Cost: $1.19

 Calories per Serving: 112

Fat: 1.4 grams

Protein: 4.7 grams

Sodium: 65.1 mg

Carbohydrates: 19.6 grams

Cholesterol: 33.8 mg

¼ cup cooked spinach

¼ cup cooked barley

1 whole egg

1 egg white

½ teaspoon extra-virgin olive oil

1 teaspoon dry white wine

½ cup semolina flour

½ cup unbleached all-purpose flour

Pinch of iodized salt

1. In a blender or food processor, purée the spinach and barley, then add the whole egg, egg white, oil, and wine; continue to blend until thoroughly smooth.
2. Sift together the semolina, flour, and salt. Stir the spinach mixture into the flour mixture.
3. Bring 1 gallon of water to a boil. While the water comes to a boil, form gnocchi mix into ½-teaspoon oval-shaped dumplings. (You can make grooved imprints on them with a fork if you like.) Drop the gnocchi into the boiling water and cook for approximately 8 minutes, until al dente.

Preparing Dough

Whenever preparing any type of dough, use flour to prevent sticking. However, you don't want a lot of excess flour on the final product, so be certain to brush all the flour off before cooking. For an easy way to create the traditional gnocchi shape, gently press the gnocchi against floured fork tines and roll the gnocchi down the fork.

Vegetable Tamale with Epazote

 Serves 6

1 red pepper

1 yellow onion

1 zucchini

¼ cup button mushrooms (leave whole)

1 tablespoon extra-virgin olive oil

½ cup Chicken or Turkey Stock (see recipes in Chapter 7)

1 cup masa harina

Fresh-cracked black pepper, to taste

Pinch of iodized salt

1 tablespoon chopped epazote (marjoram or cilantro can be substituted)

6 corn husks (soaked in water for at least 1 hour, then drained)

Masa harina is a very fine corn flour, available at most health food stores or Spanish markets.

1. Slice the pepper in half, then remove and discard the seeds and stem. Cut the onion into 1-inch-thick rings. Slice the zucchini thickly lengthwise. Lightly oil all the vegetables, then grill or roast them al dente (approximately 10 minutes).
2. In a medium-size bowl, mix together the stock, masa, remaining oil, black pepper, salt, and epazote.
3. Lay out the corn husks. Place a layer of the masa mixture in the husks, then add the vegetables, and then another layer of masa mix. Roll up the tamales tightly and tie the ends closed with small strips of husk.
4. Bring water to boil in a steamer pan. Place the tamales in the perforated pan and steam for 20 to 30 minutes.

Epazote

Epazote is a Mexican herb with a very distinct flavor. It is used to season beans, soups, salads, and a variety of other dishes. Epazote can be found in most Mexican or Latin grocery stores. If you cannot find it, you can leave it out of the recipe, but you should use more of the other seasonings to balance out the flavor.

Artichoke Rice Bake

 Serves 6

Total Cost: $5.42

Calories per Serving: 162

Fat: 4.4 grams

Protein: 5.0 grams

Sodium: 203.3 mg

Carbohydrates: 26.4 grams

Cholesterol: 1.1 mg

3 fresh artichokes

1 shallot

2 cloves garlic

2 teaspoons olive oil

½ cup brown rice

2½ cups Basic Vegetable Stock (Chapter 7)

3 ounces soft tofu

1 sprig fresh tarragon

Fresh-cracked black pepper, to taste

6 green olives

6 black olives

½ cup Balsamic Reduction (see recipe in Chapter 5)

1. Trim the top of each artichoke leaf with scissors and cut the artichokes in half lengthwise. Peel the stems and remove the prickly "choke" in the centers. Cook in boiling water for 15 minutes, then remove and let cool. Cut the shallot into a small dice and mince the garlic.
2. Heat 1 teaspoon of the oil to low temperature in a medium-size saucepan; add the shallots and garlic, and sweat for 2 minutes. Add the rice; stir for 1 minute. Add 2 cups of the stock, cover, and simmer on medium heat for 35 to 40 minutes.
3. Preheat oven to 350°F.
4. In a medium-size bowl, combine the cooked rice mixture with the tofu, tarragon, pepper, and olives. Place the artichokes in a baking dish. Stuff small amounts of the rice mix between the artichoke leaves. Pour the remaining stock into the baking dish. Drizzle the remaining oil over the top of the artichokes. Cover and bake for 20 minutes. Serve with Balsamic Reduction sauce.

Focaccia

 Serves 6

 Total Cost: $1.61

Calories per Serving: 151

Fat: 1.2 grams

Protein: 4.0 grams

Sodium: 83.3 mg

Carbohydrates: 30.6 grams

Cholesterol: 0 mg

1 teaspoon olive oil

½ cup rye flour

1½ cups all-purpose
    unbleached flour

½ teaspoon baking powder

½ teaspoon baking soda

¾ cup water

1. Preheat oven to 375°F. Brush a small loaf or cake pan with some of the oil.
2. Mix together the remaining oil and all the other ingredients. Dust a work area with flour, and knead the dough for 10 to 15 minutes. Place in the pan and let rise for at least 1 hour in a warm place.
3. Place the pan in the oven and bake for 45 minutes or until golden brown.

Savory Israeli Couscous Carrot Cake

 Serves 6

$ Total Cost: $1.18

Calories per Serving: 186

Fat: 2.7 grams

Protein: 7.6 grams

Sodium: 207.4 mg

Carbohydrates: 34.7 grams

Cholesterol: 35.3 mg

1½ teaspoons olive oil

6 carrots

1 shallot

2 sprigs rosemary, leaves only

1 whole egg

1 egg white

1 cup cooked couscous

¼ cup skim milk

1½ cups whole-wheat flour

½ teaspoon baking powder

¼ teaspoon iodized salt

1. Preheat oven to 375°F. Brush a 8-inch layer-cake pan with a quarter of the oil.
2. Peel and grate the carrots. Mince the shallot.
3. Combine the carrots and shallots with the rosemary, whole egg, egg white, cooked couscous, the remaining oil, and the milk. In a separate bowl, sift together the flour, baking powder, and salt. Slowly stir dry mixture into the wet mixture.
4. Place in the prepared cake pan and bake for 45 minutes. The cake is ready when golden brown or when the center of the cake comes out clean on a toothpick. Let the cake cool for a few minutes before serving.

Bulgur-Stuffed Zucchini

 Serves 6

 Total Cost: $4.77

Calories per Serving: 109

Fat: 2 grams

Protein: 2.8 grams

Sodium: 32.7 mg

Carbohydrates: 18.6 grams

Cholesterol: 0 mg

1 shallot

1 medium tomato

3 cloves garlic

2 leeks

3 small zucchini

2 teaspoons extra-virgin
  olive oil

1 cup bulgur wheat

½ cup dry white wine

3 cups Basic Vegetable Stock
  (see recipe in Chapter 7)

½ cup fresh mint

½ cup fresh parsley

1 teaspoon grated lemon zest

1. Preheat oven to 375°F.
2. Finely dice the shallot and tomato. Mince the garlic and thinly slice the leeks. Cut the zucchini in half lengthwise and place the halves in a microwave-safe dish, cut-side down. Pour in just enough water to cover the bottom of the dish and par-cook in the microwave for 1 to 2 minutes on high heat; let cool slightly.
3. Heat the oil to medium temperature in a medium-size stock-pot. Add the shallot, garlic, and bulgur; toss in the oil until slightly brown, about 5 minutes. Add the leeks and let them wilt in the mixture. Pour in the wine and let reduce for about 1 minute.
4. Add the stock and simmer for approximately 15 minutes, until the bulgur is thoroughly cooked.
5. Meanwhile, chop the mint and parsley. When the bulgur is cooked, remove from heat and stir in the tomato, mint, parsley, and lemon zest.
6. Spoon the mixture into the zucchini halves and place on baking sheet; bake in the oven until the zucchini is reheated, about 5 to 8 minutes.

Risotto Patties

 Serves 6

Total Cost: $3.78

Calories per Serving: 269

Fat: 8.5 grams

Protein: 9.6 grams

Sodium: 258.6 mg

Carbohydrates: 36.8 grams

Cholesterol: 13.6 mg

1 shallot

1 leek

2 cups mushrooms (any single variety or mixed)

2 tablespoons olive oil

1½ cups arborio rice

¼ cup dry white wine

4¼ cups stock (flavor of your choice; see Chapter 7 for recipes)

4 ounces Manchego cheese (Parmesan can be substituted)

Fresh-cracked black pepper, to taste

1. Chop the shallot. Finely dice the whole leek and roughly chop the mushrooms.
2. Heat 1½ tablespoons of the oil to medium temperature in a medium-size saucepan. Add the shallots, leeks, and mushrooms; sauté for approximately 3 minutes. Add the rice, and toss in mixture.
3. Add the wine and let fully incorporate into rice mixture. Add the stock ¼ cup at a time, letting each become fully absorbed before adding the next, until the rice is thoroughly cooked. Add the cheese and pepper.
4. Let cool, then form into patties. Heat the remaining oil to medium-high temperature in a medium-size saucepan; brown the patties on both sides.

Arborio Rice

If you want to stick to the classic Italian risotto, you must use arborio rice. This rice gives the risotto its creamy texture.

Browned Mixed Potato Pancakes

 Serves 6

$ Total Cost: $0.75

Calories per Serving: 57

Fat: 2.2 grams

Protein: 0.7 grams

Sodium: 12.5 mg

Carbohydrates: 8.6 grams

Cholesterol: 0 mg

1 large sweet potato

1 large baking potato

1 tablespoon olive oil

1. Peel and shred the potatoes. Form into small patties. Heat a small sauté pan to medium-high heat and brush with oil. Place the potato patties in the sauté pan. Let brown on each side; serve immediately.

Pasta Dough

Serves 6

$ Total Cost: $1.56

Calories per Serving: 178

Fat: 3.3 grams

Protein: 6.1 grams

Sodium: 20.6 mg

Carbohydrates: 29.9 grams

Cholesterol: 33.8 mg

¾ cup semolina flour

1 cup unbleached all-purpose flour

Pinch of iodized salt

1 whole egg

1 egg white

1 tablespoon extra-virgin olive oil

½ tablespoon cold water

Cooking time varies according to thickness of dough; thicker dough needs to cook longer.

1. Sift together semolina, all-purpose flour, and salt. In a separate bowl, whisk whole egg and egg white; then mix in the oil and water.
2. Combine dry and wet ingredients and mix with dough hook at medium speed 2 minutes until a ball forms. Let dough rest 1 hour in refrigerator.
3. Roll out and form as desired.
4. Bring 1 gallon of water to a boil and cook dough al dente (approximately 4 to 8 minutes). Serve immediately.

CHAPTER 12
VEGETARIAN ENTRÉES

Yellow Squash Wafers

 Serves 6

 Total Cost: $2.85

 Calories per Serving: 58.4

Fat: 2.5 grams

Protein: 1.6 grams

Sodium: 70 mg

Carbohydrates: 8.7 grams

Cholesterol: 0 mg

2 teaspoons olive oil, divided

2 medium-size yellow squashes

1 tablespoon curry powder

Fresh-cracked black pepper, to taste

Kosher salt, to taste

1 whole leek

¼ cup Spanish olives

¾ cup brown rice

2½ cups Basic Vegetable Stock (Chapter 7)

1. Preheat oven to 250°F.
2. Grease a baking sheet with some of the olive oil. Very thinly slice the squashes, then place on the baking sheet and drizzle (or spray) with more oil (about half the oil). Sprinkle with curry powder, pepper, and salt. Bake 6 to 8 hours, until the squash is thoroughly dried and crisp.
3. Finely slice the whole leek and chop the olives. Heat the remaining oil in a large sauté pan; sweat the leeks until soft, then add the rice and stock. Simmer for 45 to 60 minutes, until the rice is completely cooked.
4. To serve, spoon the cooked rice onto serving plates, sprinkle with olives, and arrange the squash wafers on top.

Grilled Portobello Mushrooms

 Serves 6

 Total Cost: $3.42

 Calories per Serving: 44

Fat: 2.4 grams

Protein: 2.1 grams

Sodium: 44.1 mg

Carbohydrates: 4.7 grams

Cholesterol: 0 mg

6 portobello mushrooms

3 cloves garlic

1 tablespoon olive oil

Fresh-cracked black pepper,
   to taste

Kosher or coarse sea salt, to
   taste (optional)

1. Preheat the grill to medium temperature. Clean off the
    mushrooms with damp paper towels or a mushroom brush,
    and scrape out the black membrane on the underside of the
    cap. Mince the garlic.
2. Mix together the oil and garlic; dip each mushroom in the oil
    and place on a rack to drain. Season with salt and pepper,
    and grill on each side until fork tender.
3. To serve, slice on the bias and fan out on serving plates.

Ratatouille

 Serves 6

 Total Cost: $3.14

 Calories per Serving: 48

Fat: 0.7 grams

Protein: 2.1 grams

Sodium: 20.6 mg

Carbohydrates: 10.1 grams

Cholesterol: 0 mg

1 small eggplant

1 small zucchini squash

1 small yellow squash

½ leek

1 plum tomato

1 shallot

2 cloves garlic

2 sprigs marjoram

¼ cup kalamata olives

½ teaspoon olive oil

1 cup Basic Vegetable Stock
(see recipe in Chapter 7)

Fresh-cracked black pepper,
to taste

1. Large-dice the eggplant, zucchini, yellow squash, leek, and tomato. Finely dice the shallot and garlic. Mince the marjoram and chop the olives.
2. Place all the ingredients in a saucepot and cook at low temperature for 1½ hours.

Summer and Winter Squash

You will often hear yellow squash referred to as "summer squash." Squash is normally divided into two groups: summer squash and winter squash. Summer squashes have thin skins and soft seeds. Winter squashes have tough skins and hard seeds.

Roasted Beets

 Serves 6

Total Cost: $1.94

Calories per Serving: 153

Fat: 11.2 grams

Protein: 1.9 grams

Sodium: 325 mg

Carbohydrates: 12.1 grams

Cholesterol: 0 mg

3 large beets (with tops)

¼ cup olive oil

1 teaspoon kosher salt

¼ cup golden or white raisins

¼ cup balsamic vinegar

¼ cup slivered almonds

Fresh-cracked black pepper, to taste

1. Preheat oven to 400°F.
2. Remove the green beet tops and thoroughly clean the beets and greens. Toss the (unpeeled) beets in the olive oil, sprinkle the salt on a baking sheet, and place the beets on top; roast for 1 to 1½ hours, until beets are fork tender.
3. While the beets roast, slice the beet greens and steam quickly in a small amount of water.
4. In a separate sauté pan, plump the raisins in balsamic vinegar by heating on medium temperature for approximately 3 minutes. Keep warm.
5. Mix together beet greens with raisins, almonds, and pepper. Peel and thinly slice the roasted beets. Fan the beets in a circle on a serving plate and mound the greens mixture in the center.

Savory Cauliflower Custard

 Serves 6

 Total Cost: $1.19

 Calories per Serving: 68

Fat: 3.9 grams

Protein: 4.1 grams

Sodium: 88.9 mg

Carbohydrates: 4.5 grams

Cholesterol: 69.9 mg

½ pound fresh cauliflower

1 tablespoon olive oil

1 sprig rosemary, leaves only

Fresh-cracked black pepper, to taste

2 eggs

1 cup skim milk

1 teaspoon all-purpose unbleached flour

Salt, to taste

1. Preheat oven to 375°F. Grease a 1-quart casserole pan.
2. Cut the cauliflower into bite-size portions, then toss in half of the oil and sprinkle with rosemary and pepper. Roast al dente, approximately 20 minutes. Allow to cool.
3. Mix together the eggs, milk, and flour. Add the cooled cauliflower to the egg mixture, then pour it into the casserole pan; bake for 15 minutes. Lightly stir the mixture and return it to the oven; bake for 15 minutes longer or until the egg mixture is completely set. Sprinkle with salt and serve.

Sautéed Fennel with Olives and Arugula

 Serves 4

 Total Cost: $5.48

 Calories per Serving: 62

Fat: 1.6 grams

Protein: 2.1 grams

Sodium: 614 mg

Carbohydrates: 11.6 grams

Cholesterol: 0 mg

1 teaspoon olive oil

1 pound fennel bulb, thinly sliced

½ cup thinly sliced leek (white and pale green parts only)

½ cup seeded and diced red bell pepper (about ½-inch dice)

¼ cup capers, rinsed and drained

¼ cup sliced kalamata olives

1½ cups arugula leaves (organic baby arugula leaves if possible)

½ teaspoon salt

Fresh-cracked black pepper, to taste

1. Heat the oil in a large nonstick skillet over medium-high heat. Add the fennel, leek, red pepper, and capers; sauté until crisp-tender, about 3 to 4 minutes.
2. Add the olives and arugula leaves, and sauté until the leaves just start to wilt, about 1 minute. Season with salt and pepper. Serve hot.

The $7 a Meal Mediterranean Cookbook

Polenta Bake

 Serves 6

Total Cost: $3.06	
Calories per Serving: 364	
Fat: 18.4 grams	
Protein: 17.3 grams	
Sodium: 936.2 mg	
Carbohydrates: 32.7 grams	
Cholesterol: 80.6 mg	

1 cup uncooked coarse-ground cornmeal

3 cups water

½ cup milk

1 teaspoon salt

1 egg

1 tablespoon butter

2 ounces cream cheese

¼ cup grated Parmesan cheese

1 cup shredded mozzarella cheese

1 tablespoon olive oil

1 8-ounce can tomato sauce

3 cloves garlic, sliced

½ teaspoon dried oregano

2 fresh basil leaves, chopped

1. Preheat oven to 350°F.
2. Over medium heat, cook cornmeal in salted water and milk, stirring with a wooden spoon or whisk until cooked and creamy, about 10 minutes.
3. Add egg and beat in completely, followed by butter, cream cheese, Parmesan cheese, and half of the mozzarella.
4. Grease a 9" × 13" baking dish with some of the olive oil; pour in polenta mixture.
5. Drizzle remaining olive oil over polenta, and then pour tomato sauce over it. Sprinkle garlic, herbs, and remaining mozzarella over top. Bake 25 minutes.

Corn Pudding

 Serves 6

3 ears corn

2 cloves garlic

1 teaspoon olive oil

¼ teaspoon dried red pepper
 flakes

Kosher salt, to taste

3 eggs

1 cup skim milk

1. Preheat the grill to medium temperature.
2. Husk the corn. Mince the garlic, and mix together with the oil and pepper flakes. Paint the corn with the seasoned oil (reserve enough oil to grease casserole dish), then sprinkle with salt; grill for 3 to 5 minutes, until the corn is completely cooked (be certain to turn the corn frequently to avoid burning). Cool thoroughly and remove kernels from cobs.
3. Preheat oven to 350°F.
4. Grease a large casserole dish with the reserved seasoned oil. In a large mixing bowl, combine the corn with the remaining ingredients, and pour into the prepared dish; bake until the pudding begins to set (about 30 minutes), then turn it lightly with a wooden spoon and return to oven to continue baking until completely set (about 30 minutes more).

Custards and Puddings

Custards and puddings can be prepared on top of the stove as well as in the oven. However, baking them in the oven in a water bath allows for a smoother and creamier texture. A water bath is a pan with sides at least 1½ to 2 inches high filled halfway with water in which the casserole dish is placed. The hot water provides a constant heat source and ensures even cooking.

The $7 a Meal Mediterranean Cookbook

Steamed Greens with Balsamic Raisin Reduction

 Serves 6

$ Total Cost: $6.64

Calories per Serving: 154

Fat: 2.1 grams

Protein: 3 grams

Sodium: 47.4 mg

Carbohydrates: 30 grams

Cholesterol: 4.3 mg

6 cups greens (kale, collard, mustard, carrot tops, or turnip greens)

1 recipe Balsamic Reduction (see recipe in Chapter 5)

½ cup golden raisins

1. Wash and slice the greens. Place in a pot with tight-fitting lid, or in a steamer, with 1 cup of water. Cover and steam for 2 to 3 minutes.
2. Heat the Balsamic Reduction and raisins, just until warm. Place the greens on the plate and drizzle with the sauce.

Vegetarian Hash

 Serves 6

$ Total Cost: $4.35

Calories per Serving: 165

Fat: 0.9 grams

Protein: 3.9 grams

Sodium: 26.1 mg

Carbohydrates: 37 grams

Cholesterol: 0 mg

1½ pounds potatoes

1 poblano (or other mild chili pepper)

2 red peppers

2 ears corn (or 1 cup corn kernels)

1 red onion

½ teaspoon olive oil

1 tablespoon chili powder

Fresh-cracked black pepper, to taste

¼ cup fresh cilantro

Kosher or coarse sea salt, to taste (optional)

1. Preheat oven to 400°F.
2. Peel and large-dice the potatoes. Cut the poblano and red peppers in half and remove the seeds. Remove corn kernels from ears. Thickly slice the onion.
3. Toss the potatoes, peppers, corn, and onions in oil, then drain on rack. Place each vegetable on a separate baking sheet and season with chili powder and black pepper; roast until fork tender. (Times will vary; check at 5-minute intervals.)
4. Chop the cilantro. Cut the peppers and onions into large dice. Combine the potatoes, peppers, corn, onions, and cilantro. Season with salt, and serve.

Potato Gnocchi

Serves 6

 Total Cost: $3.60

 Calories per Serving: 224

Fat: 5.4 grams

Protein: 9.2 grams

Sodium: 205.7 mg

Carbohydrates: 33.7 grams

Cholesterol: 10.7 mg

1 medium potato

1½ cups all-purpose flour

2 egg whites

¼ cup Basic Vegetable Stock (see recipe in Chapter 7)

Pinch of iodized salt

1 teaspoon olive oil

2 cups Fresh Tomato Sauce (see recipe in Chapter 5)

2 ounces Romano cheese

3 large basil leaves

Fresh-cracked black pepper, to taste

1. Peel the whole potato and boil until thoroughly cooked, about 20 minutes.
2. Using a dough hook set at low speed (or your hands), mix together the flour, potato, egg whites, stock, salt, and oil for 1 minute until all the ingredients are thoroughly incorporated; let the dough rest for approximately 1 hour.
3. Roll out the dough using both hands to form a long ½-inch-thick "rope," then slice into 1-inch-long pieces. Drop the pasta in salted boiling water and cook al dente, then drain.
4. Heat the sauce. Grate the cheese and thinly slice the basil. To serve, ladle the sauce over the top of the gnocchi, then sprinkle with black pepper, cheese, and basil.

Pasta Dishes

Pasta is a common staple in the Italian diet. Many variations can be created by the substitution of ingredients and with the shape of the pasta. Gnocchi is no exception. It can be prepared in diverse ways as well. To obtain the optimum flavor, toss the cooked gnocchi in a sauté pan with the sauce for 1 to 2 minutes.

Skewered Vegetables

 Serves 6

 Total Cost: $3.11

 Calories per Serving: 77

Fat: 0.9 grams

Protein: 1.8 grams

Sodium: 59.2 mg

Carbohydrates: 16.1 grams

Cholesterol: 0 mg

1 medium par-baked sweet potato or yam

1 medium par-baked baking potato

1 yellow pepper

1 medium-size red onion

1 medium zucchini

1 sprig tarragon, leaves only

1 teaspoon olive oil

Fresh-cracked black pepper, to taste

Kosher salt, to taste

1. Soak 12 wooden skewers in water for at least 4 hours.
2. Peel and cut the potatoes into 2-inch cubes. Stem and seed the pepper, and cut it into 2-inch squares. Cut the onion into wedges. Cut the zucchini into 2-inch chunks and mince the tarragon.
3. Preheat grill.
4. String the vegetables on the skewers, alternating types. Brush the skewered vegetables with the oil, sprinkle with pepper and salt, and grill until the vegetables are cooked al dente. Sprinkle with tarragon before serving.

Par-baking Potatoes

Wash the potatoes. Lightly coat them with oil and cook in a 400°F oven for 1 hour. The potatoes should feel slightly hard as they are only 75% done. Let them cool and refridgerate them overnight. When grilling the potatoes, they will be done when they have a golden brown color and have almost the same texture as French fries.

Vegetable Terrine

 Serves 6

1 medium-size baked sweet potato

1 large par-baked baking potato

1 medium-size yellow onion

3 red bell peppers

1 large eggplant

4 cloves garlic

1 head escarole

2 tablespoons olive oil

Fresh-cracked black pepper, to taste

1 tablespoon curry powder

¼ cup chopped unsalted cashew nuts

1. Preheat oven to 375°F.
2. Peel and mash the sweet potato. Peel and slice the baking potato into 1-inch-thick slices. Thickly slice the onion. Cut the peppers in half and remove the seeds. Slice the eggplant lengthwise into 1-inch slices. Mince the garlic. Steam the escarole for about 7 or 8 minutes.
3. Brush the onion, peppers, and eggplant with half of the oil, then sprinkle with black pepper and ½ tablespoon of curry powder. Roast in oven until al dente, approximately 10 to 20 minutes.
4. Grease a loaf pan with half of the remaining oil. Line the pan with the eggplant, allowing the slices to drape up and over the sides of the pan. Then layer the remainder of the ingredients and sprinkle with remaining curry powder. Drizzle with oil. Fold over the eggplant slices to seal the terrine.
5. Seal tightly with plastic wrap and place something heavy on top to press the ingredients firmly together. Refrigerate at least 4 hours.
6. Cut into 2-inch slices to serve.

Zucchini Parmesan

 Serves 6

 Total Cost: $3.64

Calories per Serving: 169

Fat: 7.1 grams

Protein: 12.8 grams

Sodium: 351.6 mg

Carbohydrates: 13.9 grams

Cholesterol: 21.3 mg

3 medium zucchini

2 egg whites

1 cup skim milk

1 teaspoon olive oil

½ cup bread crumbs

2 cups Long-Cooking Traditional Tomato Sauce (see recipe in Chapter 5)

6 ounces part-skim mozzarella cheese, shredded

Fresh-cracked black pepper, to taste

You may use plain or preseasoned bread crumbs for this recipe. Also, try adding thin-sliced fresh basil or chopped oregano for flair and extra flavor.

1. Preheat oven to 375°F.
2. Slice the zucchini into ½-inch-thick coins. Beat the egg whites and mix with the milk. Brush a baking sheet with the oil. Dip the zucchini into the egg mixture, then into the bread crumbs, and shake off excess; place on baking sheet and bake for 10 to 15 minutes, until the zucchini are just fork tender.
3. Ladle enough sauce into a large casserole or baking dish to cover the bottom. Cover the bottom of the dish with a single layer of zucchini, then top with the cheese, then sauce. Repeat the process until you have used all the ingredients; bake for 5 to 10 minutes, until the cheese has melted and begins to brown on top.

Parmesan

Parmesan is best known as a type of cheese, but the term "Parmesan" also loosely refers to a type of cooking—for example, Chicken Parmesan. Any type of Parmesan dish indicates the presence of some type of cheese, but not necessarily Parmesan cheese.

The $7 a Meal Mediterranean Cookbook

Squash and Goat Cheese Napoleon

Serves 6

Total Cost: $5.69

Calories per Serving: 162

Fat: 11.4 grams

Protein: 7.5 grams

Sodium: 208.3 mg

Carbohydrates: 6.8 grams

Cholesterol: 22.1 mg

1 medium-size yellow squash

1 medium zucchini squash

1 tablespoon olive oil

1 leek

1 cup fresh spinach

3 cloves garlic

¼ cup pitted, black olives, chopped

2 plum tomatoes

¼ cup dry red wine

½ cup Red Wine Vegetable Stock (see recipe in Chapter 7)

Fresh-cracked black pepper, to taste

6 ounces goat cheese, crumbled

1. Heat grill to medium-high temperature.
2. Slice the squashes lengthwise. Coat a pan with some of the olive oil and grill the squashes for approximately 1 to 2 minutes on each side until al dente.
3. Thinly slice the leek and spinach. Mince the garlic and olives. Dice the tomatoes.
4. Heat the remaining oil to medium temperature in a large saucepan. Add the leek and garlic; sauté for 2 minutes. Add the spinach; sauté 1 more minute. Add the tomatoes, and sauté for 1 minute. Add the wine and stock, and reduce by half.
5. To serve, layer the ingredients, starting with squashes, then leek mixture, then pepper, olives, and goat cheese, repeating until you've used all the ingredients.

Vegetable Samosas

Serves 6

DOUGH

¼ cup whole-wheat flour

½ cup all-purpose unbleached flour

4 tablespoons olive oil

1–3 tablespoons ice water

VEGETABLE STUFFING

1 potato

1 large yellow onion

2 cloves garlic

1 teaspoon virgin olive oil

1 teaspoon curry powder

½ cup Basic Vegetable Stock (see recipe in Chapter 7)

1 2-ounce can chickpeas

¼ cup cooked green peas

¼ cup cooked spinach

Fresh-cracked black pepper, to taste

Kosher salt, to taste

1. Prepare the dough by mixing the flours, 3 tablespoons oil, and ice water, 1 teaspoon at a time; dough will look like bread crumbs. Refrigerate the dough while you prepare the stuffing.
2. Peel and dice the potato and onion. Mince the garlic. Heat 1 teaspoon virgin olive oil to medium temperature in a small saucepan. Add the potatoes, onions, garlic, and curry powder; sauté for 5 minutes, then add the stock and simmer until the potatoes are fork tender. Remove from heat.
3. Mix the potato mixture with both peas and the spinach. Season to taste with pepper and salt. Allow the mixture to thoroughly cool.
4. Preheat oven to 400°F. Brush a baking sheet with the remaining olive oil.
5. Roll the dough into 4-inch circles and place a heaping table-spoonful of vegetable mix in the center of each. Fold the dough circles in half and thoroughly seal; place on prepared baking sheet and bake for 8 to 12 minutes until golden brown.

Braised Okra with Tomato

 Serves 6

Total Cost: $4.97

Calories per Serving: 132

Fat: 6.7 grams

Protein: 6 grams

Sodium: 220.2 mg

Carbohydrates: 12.4 grams

Cholesterol: 16.6 mg

1½ pounds okra

8 plum tomatoes

2 shallots

4 cloves garlic

1 tablespoon olive oil

¼ cup dry red wine

½ cup Basic Vegetable Stock (see recipe in Chapter 7)

4 sprigs oregano, leaves only

4 ounces feta cheese, crumbled

Fresh-cracked black pepper, to taste

1. Preheat oven to 375°F.
2. Remove the tops of the okra. Cut the tomatoes into wedges. Fine-dice the shallots and mince the garlic.
3. Heat the oil in a Dutch oven (or other heavy-bottomed pan with a lid) to medium-high temperature. Add the okra, tomatoes, shallots, and garlic; sauté for 2 minutes. Add the wine, and reduce by half. Add the stock and oregano. Bring to simmer, cover, and place in the oven for 15 to 20 minutes.
4. Remove from oven and add the feta and pepper. Adjust seasoning to taste, then serve.

Caramelized Onion Tart

Serves 6

Total Cost: $1.93

Calories per Serving: 146

Fat: 7.2 grams

Protein: 2.3 grams

Sodium: 6.5 mg

Carbohydrates: 16.8 grams

Cholesterol: 5 mg

CRUST

¼ cup whole-wheat flour

½ cup unbleached all-purpose flour

2 tablespoons olive oil

1–3 tablespoons water

FILLING

1 medium Vidalia onion or yellow onion

1 medium-size red onion

2 shallots

1 leek

1 teaspoon olive oil

¼ cup dry red wine

1 tablespoon cold unsalted butter

3 sprigs thyme, leaves only

Fresh-cracked black pepper, to taste

1. Preheat oven to 400°F.
2. Prepare the crust by mixing together the flours and olive oil. Add the water 1 tablespoonful at a time until the dough clumps together. Knead, then roll out thin and place in tart or pie pan. Partially bake, about 15 minutes.
3. Prepare the filling by finely slicing the onions, shallots, and leek. Heat the oil in a large sauté pan over low to medium heat. Add the onions, shallots, and leeks; sweat, covered, for 15 minutes.
4. Increase heat to medium-high temperature and add the wine; reduce by half. Add the butter, thyme, and pepper.
5. Spoon the onion mixture into the tart shell and bake for 15 minutes. Slice and serve.

Blind Baking

You can "blind bake" pie shells when they have an unbaked filling, such as pudding, or to help ensure that they stay crisp. Prepare 2 shells—1 is the pie shell you will use, the other is a tin foil shell that lines the pie shell and is filled with rice or dried beans. The second shell helps keep the pie shell's shape when baking. Place the filled shell on top of the other and bake until almost done. Then remove and allow the first pie shell to finish baking by itself.

Artichokes Stuffed with Risotto

 Serves 10

 Total Cost: $6.78

 Calories per Serving: 224

Fat: 3.9 grams

Protein: 6.5 grams

Sodium: 129.7 mg

Carbohydrates: 39.8 grams

Cholesterol: 4.4 mg

5 artichokes

2 tablespoons olive oil, divided

2 large leeks

½ bulb garlic

2 cups arborio rice

½ cup dry white wine (not cooking wine)

5½ cups stock of choice (see recipes in Chapter 7)

½ cup ricotta cheese

1 tablespoon red pepper flakes (optional)

3 anchovy fillets, mashed (optional)

1. Prepare the artichokes by cutting each in half lengthwise, leaving the stem on. Snip off the pointy ends of each leaf. Peel the outer skin of the stem. Remove the "choke" (the purplish-white center) and discard. Parboil the artichokes for about 15 minutes and quickly submerge them in ice water.
2. Preheat oven to 375°F. Lightly grease a baking sheet with 1 tablespoon of the oil. Thoroughly clean and finely dice the leeks, using both the white and green parts. Peel and mince the garlic.
3. Heat the remaining oil to medium temperature in a large saucepan. Add the leeks, garlic, and rice. Stir for 2 minutes. Add the wine, and stir until completely absorbed. Add the stock ½ cup at a time, stirring frequently and allowing each addition to be completely absorbed before adding the next. Continue until all the stock is absorbed and the rice is tender.
4. Remove from heat, and stir in the ricotta. Stuff each artichoke leaf with the risotto, and place on the prepared baking sheet. Bake for 20 minutes.
5. Top with red pepper flakes and anchovy, if desired, and serve.

Asparagi alla Milanese (Milan-Style Asparagus)

 Serves 4

2 cups water

2 pounds asparagus

1 egg

3 tablespoons unsalted butter

¼ cup fresh-grated Parmesan cheese

1. Bring the water to a boil in a large saucepan. Break off the "woody" ends of the asparagus (holding each spear at each end and bending until the asparagus spear breaks).
2. Place the asparagus in a steamer insert, cover, and steam al dente. While the asparagus is steaming, fry the egg.
3. Remove the asparagus from the water, drain, and place on a serving platter. Place pats of the butter on top and evenly distribute the butter over the asparagus as it melts. Place the fried egg over the asparagus tips. Serve sprinkled with the cheese.

Italian Vegetable Bake

 Serves: 6

1 28-ounce can tomatoes, coarsely chopped, juices reserved

1 onion, sliced

½ pound green beans, sliced

½ pound okra, cut into ½-inch lengths

¾ cup finely chopped green bell peppers

2 tablespoons lemon juice

1 tablespoon chopped fresh basil

1½ teaspoons fresh oregano leaves, chopped

3 medium zucchini, cut into 1-inch cubes

1 eggplant, peeled and cut into 1-inch chunks

2 tablespoons grated Parmesan cheese

1. Preheat oven to 325°F.
2. In a baking dish, combine the tomatoes and their liquid, onion, green beans, okra, bell peppers, lemon juice, basil, and oregano. Cover with foil or a lid.
3. Bake for 15 minutes. Mix in the zucchini and eggplant, cover, and continue to bake, stirring occasionally, until the vegetables are tender, about 1 hour. Sprinkle the top with Parmesan cheese just before serving.

Italian Green Beans with Potatoes

 Serves 6

$ Total Cost: $3.97

Calories per Serving: 125

Fat: 5.2 grams

Protein: 3.3 grams

Sodium: 5.7 mg

Carbohydrates: 18.4 grams

Cholesterol: 0 mg

2 baked potatoes

2 cloves garlic

1¼ pounds Italian green beans

1 tablespoon olive oil

½ cup Basic Vegetable Stock (see recipe in Chapter 7)

¼ cup chopped walnuts

½ teaspoon dried oregano

½ teaspoon dried marjoram

Fresh-cracked black pepper, to taste

1. Peel and dice the cooled baked potatoes. Mince the garlic. Remove the stems from the beans.
2. Heat the oil to medium temperature in a large saucepan. Add the garlic and beans, toss gently, then add the potatoes, stock, nuts, oregano, marjoram, and pepper; simmer for approximately 8 minutes. Adjust seasoning to taste before serving.

Mushroom Ravioli with Walnut-Parsley Pesto

 Serves 6

 Total Cost: $5.48

 Calories per Serving: 455

Fat: 30.5 grams

Protein: 9.6 grams

Sodium: 170.5 mg

Carbohydrates: 32.2 grams

Cholesterol: 38 mg

2 shallots

2 cloves garlic

2 portobello mushrooms

1 tablespoon olive oil

¼ cup dry white wine

1 teaspoon unsalted cold butter

Fresh-cracked black pepper, to taste

12 ounces Pasta Dough (see recipe in Chapter 11)

1 cup Walnut-Parsley Pesto (see recipe in Chapter 5)

1. Finely dice the shallots and mince the garlic. Clean off the mushrooms with damp paper towels, scrape out the black membrane on the underside of the cap, and cut them into a large dice.

2. Heat the oil to medium temperature in a large sauté pan. Add the shallots, garlic, and mushrooms; sauté for approximately 5 minutes. Add the wine and let it reduce by half. Add the butter and remove from heat. Season with pepper and allow to cool thoroughly.

3. Roll the pasta dough at least 1/16-inch thick and cut into 3- to 4-inch squares or circles. On one side of each square, add 1 tablespoon of the mushroom mixture. Fold each ravioli in half and seal tightly with a fork.

4. Bring 2 quarts of water to a boil in a large saucepot. Cook the ravioli al dente (approximately 5 to 7 minutes), then drain and serve with the pesto.

Exotic Mushrooms

Exotic mushrooms can be substituted for everyday mushrooms in many recipes. They are most often found in dried form, so all you have to do is rehydrate them before use. To rehydrate dried mushrooms, soak each ½ ounce in ½ cup hot tap water for about 10 minutes. The mushrooms will retain their texture but lose most of their flavor. The liquid, which inherits all the mushrooms' flavors, can be used in the recipe.

Pasta with Arugula and Brie

 Serves 6

Total Cost: $3.71
Calories per Serving: 357
Fat: 7.8 grams
Protein: 14.6 grams
Sodium: 146.8 mg
Carbohydrates: 56 grams
Cholesterol: 21.9 mg

4 heads arugula

6 ounces Brie cheese

1¼ pounds pasta

1 teaspoon extra-virgin olive
   oil

Fresh-cracked black pepper,
   to taste

1. Wash arugula in cold water. Carefully remove leaves and tear into bite-size pieces. Cut the Brie into small pieces (since Brie is very soft, shape does not matter).
2. Cook the pasta al dente; drain. Just as the pasta is done, toss all the ingredients together in a bowl. Serve as is (the heat from the cooked pasta will wilt the arugula and melt the Brie adequately).

Pomodori Ripieni (Stuffed Roma Tomatoes)

Serves 10

 Total Cost: $2.45

 Calories per Serving: 104

Fat: 3.9 grams

Protein: 4.2 grams

Sodium: 163.3 mg

Carbohydrates: 13.5 grams

Cholesterol: 4.5 mg

20 Roma tomatoes

4 sprigs fresh basil

3 thick slices Italian bread

½ cup shredded provolone cheese

Fresh-cracked black pepper, to taste

1 tablespoon olive oil

1. Preheat oven to 400°F. Slice the tomatoes in half and scoop out and reserve the pulp. Set aside the tomato halves. Clean and gently slice the basil. Medium-dice the bread.
2. Mix together the reserved tomato pulp, basil, bread, cheese, and pepper in a medium-sized bowl.
3. Stuff each tomato half with some of the mixture. Place on baking sheet, drizzle with oil, and sprinkle with pepper. Roast for 8 minutes. Serve immediately.

Stuffed Onions

Serves: 6

Total Cost: $6.56

Calories per Serving: 381

Fat: 11.9 grams

Protein: 6.3 grams

Sodium: 27 mg

Carbohydrates: 61.6 grams

Cholesterol: 0 mg

6 large onions

2 stalks celery

1 sprig fresh rosemary

5 sprigs fresh parsley

1 sprig fresh thyme

2 garlic cloves

2 tablespoons vegetable oil

2¼ cups long-grain rice

4 ½ cups boiling water

¼ cup pine nuts

Salt and pepper to taste

1 tablespoon olive oil

2 tablespoons balsamic vinegar

1. Peel the onions. Slice off both ends of the onions, so they are able to stand upright. Place the onions in a saucepan with enough water to cover them. Bring to a boil, then reduce the heat, cover, and let simmer for 10 to 15 minutes depending on the size and type of onion, until they are tender.

2. Using a slotted spoon, gently remove the onions and drain. When cool, gently push out the cores of the onions with your fingers, leaving the onion shell intact. Reserve the shells and cores.

3. To prepare the filling, trim and finely chop the celery, onion cores, and herbs. Peel and chop the garlic. Heat the vegetable oil in a saucepan. Add the chopped onion, celery, garlic, and herbs. Cook until the vegetables are soft but not brown. Stir frequently. Add the rice and fry it with the vegetables for 3 to 4 minutes. Pour in 4½ cups boiling water, cover, and simmer for 15 to 20 minutes, until the rice is soft and the water has been absorbed. Add the pine nuts and salt and pepper to taste.

4. Make a vinaigrette by combining 1 tablespoon olive oil and the balsamic vinegar with some salt and pepper in a bowl. Beat with a whisk.

5. Preheat the oven to 325°F. Pour the vinaigrette into the baking dish. Using a teaspoon, stuff the onions with the rice filling. Arrange the onions upright in the baking dish and cover with aluminum foil. Place in the oven and bake for 30 minutes.

Orecchiette with Summer Tomato Sauce and Olives

Serves: 5

Total Cost: $2.99

Calories per Serving: 400

Fat: 9.7 grams

Protein: 11.8 grams

Sodium: 147.8 mg

Carbohydrates: 66.4 grams

Cholesterol: 0 mg

1½ pounds tomatoes, peeled, seeded, and chopped into ½-inch pieces

1 teaspoon minced garlic

3 tablespoons olive oil

2 tablespoons shredded fresh basil leaves

Pepper to taste

1 pound orecchiette or other round or shell-shaped pasta

⅓ cup kalamata or other brine-cured black olives, pitted

1. In a large bowl, combine the tomatoes, garlic, oil, basil, and pepper. Stir to mix well. Set aside at room temperature for at least 30 minutes.
2. Cook the pasta in boiling salted water until al dente. Drain. Stir the olives into the tomato mixture, add the pasta, toss well, and serve immediately.

Pasta e Fagioli (Pasta and Bean Soup)

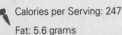

Serves 10

$ Total Cost: $4.46

Calories per Serving: 247

Fat: 5.6 grams

Protein: 4.5 grams

Sodium: 411.1 mg

Carbohydrates: 43.1 grams

Cholesterol: 4.2 mg

1 pound dried chickpeas

4 gallons Basic Vegetable Stock (see recipe in Chapter 7)

4 shallots

1 bulb garlic

2 bunches celeriac (celery root)

2 pounds plum tomatoes

½ cup fresh parsley

2 tablespoons olive oil

2 cups cooked bite-size pasta of choice

½ cup fresh-grated Asiago cheese

Fresh-cracked black pepper, to taste

1. Sort through the chickpeas, discarding any stones. In a large stockpot, simmer the peas in 2 gallons of the stock for approximately 2 to 3 hours, until the beans are tender. Drain.
2. Peel and finely chop the shallots, garlic, and celeriac. Clean and chop the tomatoes and parsley.
3. Heat the oil in a large stockpot over medium temperature. Sauté the shallots, garlic, and celeriac for 3 minutes. Add the tomatoes and sauté for 1 minute. Add the remaining stock, the chickpeas, and parsley. Let simmer for 1 hour, uncovered.
4. Just before serving, stir in the pasta. Sprinkle each serving with the cheese and pepper.

Rolled Squash

 Serves 10

 Total Cost: $4.13

Calories per Serving: 248

Fat: 19.7 grams

Protein: 7 grams

Sodium: 273.4 mg

Carbohydrates: 13.8 grams

Cholesterol: 13.8 mg

1 large eggplant

2 large zucchini

1 large yellow squash

1 medium butternut squash

Coarse salt

1½ cups cheese sauce

1 cup Basil-Nut Pesto (see recipe in Chapter 5)

1. Preheat oven to 375°F. Clean and slice the eggplant, zucchini, and yellow squash lengthwise. Peel and slice the butternut squash, scoop out the insides, and rinse the seeds. Toss the seeds in the salt and toast lightly on greased baking sheet for about 10 minutes.
2. Partially steam the butternut squash on the stovetop or in the microwave until just fork-tender. Drain off liquid.
3. Coat the inside of a loaf pan with half of the cheese sauce. Then layer the eggplant, zucchini, yellow squash, and butternut squash in the pan. Top with more cheese sauce (leave a little for the end), and ½ cup of the pesto.
4. Carefully fold over the sliced squash to form a roll and top with the remaining pesto and cheese sauce. Cover, and bake for 20 minutes.
5. Uncover, and cook for 10 minutes. Serve sprinkled with toasted seeds.

CHAPTER 13

POULTRY AND FISH

Ground Turkey Patties

 Serves 6

 Total Cost: $4.01

Calories per Serving: 248

Fat: 15.2 grams

Protein: 23.7 grams

Sodium: 181.8 mg

Carbohydrates: 4.2 grams

Cholesterol: 76.2 mg

1 cup mushrooms

1 leek (white part only)

1 pound ground turkey

¼ cup peanut butter

1 teaspoon soy sauce

½ teaspoon olive oil

¼ cup poultry Demi-Glacé Reduction Sauce (see recipe in Chapter 5)

1. Preheat oven to 350°F.
2. Clean the mushrooms with a damp paper towel. Chop the mushrooms and leek.
3. Mix together the turkey, mushrooms, leek, peanut butter, and soy sauce; form the mixture into patties.
4. Brush the oil in the bottom of a casserole pan and place the patties in the pan; cover and bake for 20 minutes.
5. Add the demi-glacé, cover, and continue baking for 10 more minutes.

Spicy Turkey Breast with Fruit Chutney

 Serves 6

 Total Cost: $6.76

Calories per Serving: 190

Fat: 4.1 grams

Protein: 19.6 grams

Sodium: 81.8 mg

Carbohydrates: 18.7 grams

Cholesterol: 48.3 mg

2 jalapeño chili peppers

2 cloves garlic

1 tablespoon olive oil

2 teaspoons all-purpose flour

Fresh-cracked black pepper, to taste

1½ pounds whole boneless turkey breast

1 shallot

1 lemon

2 pears

1 tablespoon honey

1. Preheat oven to 350°F.
2. Stem, seed, and mince the peppers. Mince the garlic. In a blender, purée the chili peppers, garlic, and oil. Mix together the flour and black pepper.
3. Spray a rack with cooking spray. Dredge the turkey in the flour mixture, then dip it in the pepper mixture, and place on rack. Cover loosely with foil and roast for 1 hour. Remove foil and brown for 10 minutes.
4. While the turkey cooks, prepare the chutney: Finely dice the shallot. Juice the lemon and grate the rind for zest. Dice the pears. Mix together the pears, shallots, lemon juice, zest, and honey.
5. Thinly slice the turkey, and serve with chutney.

Turkey Breast Piccata

 Serves 6

 Total Cost: $6.05

 Calories per Serving: 169

Fat: 4.2 grams

Protein: 20 grams

Sodium: 106.1 mg

Carbohydrates: 9.9 grams

Cholesterol: 48.4 mg

1½ pounds whole boneless turkey breast

¼ cup flour

1 lemon

¼ cup fresh parsley

1 tablespoon olive oil

¼ cup dry white wine

½ cup Turkey Stock (see recipe in Chapter 7)

½ tablespoon capers

1. Slice the turkey breast into thin scallop-size portions and dredge in the flour. Grate the lemon rind for zest and juice the lemon. Chop the parsley.
2. Heat the oil to medium-high temperature in a large sauté pan. Sauté the turkey until light golden brown, approximately 2 minutes on each side.
3. Add the wine and lemon juice, and let reduce by half. Add the stock and simmer on high temperature for 1 minute. Remove the turkey from the pan and keep warm. Allow the liquid to reduce by half.
4. To serve, sprinkle with capers and parsley, and drizzle with sauce.

Lemon Supremes

Lemon supremes can be used as a garnish. They are made by completely removing all peels and pith from the lemon and cutting out each section. Then simply arrange them on a plate to suit your artistic style.

Very Lemony Chicken

 Serves: 4

Total Cost: $5.62

Calories per Serving: 138

Fat: 2.5 grams

Protein: 27.2 grams

Sodium: 231.4 mg

Carbohydrates: 4.3 grams

Cholesterol: 66.7 mg

1 pound chicken breast, boneless, skinless

Juice of 2–3 lemons

2 tablespoons distilled white vinegar

½ cup lemon zest

1 tablespoon chopped fresh oregano or 1 teaspoon dried oregano, crumbled

1 onion, sliced

¼ teaspoon salt

⅛ teaspoon pepper

½ teaspoon paprika

1. Place the chicken in a 9" × 13" × 2" baking dish. In a small bowl, mix together the lemon juice, vinegar, lemon zest, oregano, and onion. Pour over the chicken, cover, and marinate in the refrigerator for several hours or as long as overnight, turning occasionally. Sprinkle with salt, pepper, and paprika.
2. Preheat oven to 300°F. Cover the baking dish with foil and bake for 30 minutes. Uncover and continue to bake until the juices run clear when a chicken piece is pierced, about 30 minutes longer. Serve immediately.

Winter "Fruited" Chicken

Serves 10

$ Total Cost: $5.93

Calories per Serving: 377

Fat: 13.2 grams

Protein: 34.3 grams

Sodium: 112.8 mg

Carbohydrates: 27.3 grams

Cholesterol: 100.5 mg

3 (1- to 2-pound) whole chickens

3 tart apples

3 pears

3 shallots

½ bulb garlic

3 sprigs fresh thyme

2 tablespoons olive oil

1 cup dry white wine (not cooking wine)

¼ cup walnuts

¼ cup dried fruit

2 bay leaves

1 cup apple juice

2 cups Chicken Stock (see recipe in Chapter 7)

1. Preheat oven to 350°F. Clean and cut each chicken into four serving pieces: two each of breast and wing, and two each of thigh and leg (reserve backbones for stock).
2. Clean and wedge the apples and pears. Peel and dice the shallots. Peel and mince the garlic. Clean the thyme and remove the leaves from the sprigs (discard the sprigs).
3. Heat the oil to medium-high temperature in an ovenproof pan on the stovetop. Brown the chicken pieces on all sides. Add the apples, pears, shallots, and garlic, and sauté for 1 minute. Add the remaining ingredients, and bring to a boil. Cover the pan, and immediately place in the oven.
4. Bake, covered, for 1 hour. Serve hot.

Linguine Stir-Fry with Asparagus and Garlic

Serves 6

1 pound linguine

2 tablespoons olive oil

1 pound skinless chicken breast meat, slivered

1 pound asparagus, trimmed and cut on the diagonal into 1-inch lengths

2 bell peppers, diced

4 cloves garlic, minced

¼ cup teriyaki sauce

1 cup reduced-sodium, fat-free chicken broth

1. Cook the linguine in boiling salted water until al dente.
2. Once the water is put on to boil, heat 1 tablespoon of the oil in a wok or large, deep skillet over high heat. Add the chicken and stir-fry until firm and cooked through, about 4 minutes. Remove the chicken and set aside. Add the remaining tablespoon oil to the pan. When it is hot, add the asparagus and bell peppers and stir-fry until crisp-tender, about 5 minutes. Add the garlic and stir-fry for 30 seconds. Stir in the teriyaki sauce and the broth.
3. As the pasta finishes cooking, return the chicken to the wok and heat through. Drain the pasta and toss with the chicken and sauce. Transfer to a warmed platter and serve at once.

Poached Chicken Breast

 Serves 6

$ Total Cost: $4.52

Calories per Serving: 307

Fat: 15.7 grams

Protein: 18.6 grams

Sodium: 120.3 mg

Carbohydrates: 24.9 grams

Cholesterol: 133 mg

1 leek

1 shallot

2 cloves garlic

1 carrot

1 stalk celery

1½ pounds boneless chicken
breasts

¼ cup dry white wine

1 cup Chicken Stock (see
recipe in Chapter 7)

¼ cup Compound Butter (see
recipe in Chapter 5)

1. Thinly slice the leek. Mince the shallot and garlic. Peel and
   shred the carrot. Shred the celery.
2. Place the leeks, shallots, garlic, carrots, and celery in the
   bottom of a skillet. Place the chicken breasts on top of the
   vegetables and pour in the wine and stock; bring to slow
   simmer. Cook for 10 to 15 minutes or until chicken is tender.
3. While the chicken is cooking, slice compound butter into 6
   serving pats. Serve each breast with a ladleful of cooking
   liquid and a pat of butter.

Chicken Galantine

 Serves 6

$ Total Cost: $6.08

Calories per Serving: 297

Fat: 7.5 grams

Protein: 28.8 grams

Sodium: 94.6 mg

Carbohydrates: 26.1 grams

Cholesterol: 104.5 mg

1 small whole chicken

1 shallot

2 cloves garlic

¼ cup pistachio nuts

8 dates

½ pound ground chicken

1 egg white

1 teaspoon dried oregano

1 teaspoon dried marjoram

Fresh-cracked black pepper, to taste

Kosher salt, to taste

1. Preheat oven to 325°F.
2. Carefully remove all the skin from the chicken by making a slit down the back and loosening the skin with your fingers (keep the skin intact as much as possible); set aside the skin. Remove the breast, thigh, and leg meat from the bone. Set the breast meat aside and grind the thigh and leg meat. Chop the shallot and mince the garlic. Chop the nuts and dates.
3. Mix together the ground chicken, egg white, nuts, dates, shallots, garlic, oregano, marjoram, pepper, and salt.
4. Lay out the skin, then lay the breast lengthwise at the center. Spoon the ground chicken mixture on top, and fold over the rest of the skin. Place in a loaf pan and bake for 1½ to 2 hours (when the internal temperature of the loaf reaches 170°F, it's done). Let cool, then slice.

The $7 a Meal Mediterranean Cookbook

Chicken Sausage Patties

Yields 24 patties

 Total Cost: $6.18

 Calories per Serving: 288

Fat: 18 grams

Protein: 28.8 grams

Sodium: 113.6 mg

Carbohydrates: 1.1 grams

Cholesterol: 106.8 mg

3 pounds ground turkey

1 medium yellow onion, finely minced

½ cup finely chopped Italian parsley

1 tablespoon chopped fresh sage or 2 teaspoons dry sage

6 cloves garlic, minced

1 tablespoon minced fresh ginger or 2 teaspoons dry ground ginger

2 teaspoons red pepper flakes

1 teaspoon ground cloves

1 teaspoon white pepper

4 tablespoons olive oil

1. In a large mixing bowl, combine all the ingredients except the oil; mix well by hand.
2. Form into 24 equally shaped patties that are approximately 2" × 1". Heat the oil in a large sauté pan. Sauté over medium heat for approximately 5 minutes on each side, until cooked through.

Curried Chicken Loaf

 Serves 6

1 shallot

6 cloves garlic

2 Granny Smith apples

¼ cup walnuts

6 slices toasted Italian bread

1 pound ground chicken

2 egg whites

2 tablespoons curry powder

Fresh-cracked black pepper, to taste

Kosher salt, to taste

1. Preheat oven to 350°F.
2. Mince the shallot and garlic. Peel, core, and cut the apples into large dice. Chop the walnuts. Soak the Italian bread in a small amount of water for 1 minute, then squeeze out all the water.
3. Mix together all the ingredients and form as desired on a baking sheet; bake for 1 hour. Let cool slightly, then slice and serve.

Warning

Never try to serve chicken rare or even medium-rare. All chicken must be thoroughly cooked to avoid foodborne illness.

The $7 a Meal Mediterranean Cookbook

Pesto-Baked Chicken

Serves 6

$ Total Cost: $6.66

Calories per Serving: 261

Fat: 13.7 grams

Protein: 28.1 grams

Sodium: 110.5 mg

Carbohydrates: 7.3 grams

Cholesterol: 65.2 mg

1½ pound chicken breast

¼ cup all-purpose flour

½ cup Basil-Nut Pesto (see recipe in Chapter 5)

1 teaspoon olive oil

Fresh-cracked black pepper, to taste

Kosher salt, to taste

½ cup chicken Demi-Glacé Reduction Sauce (see recipe in Chapter 5)

1. Preheat oven to 375°F.
2. Remove the skin from the chicken and cut the chicken into serving portions. Toss the pieces in flour, then dredge in pesto.
3. Place the chicken on an oiled rack in a roasting pan. Season with pepper and salt, and bake for 1 to 1½ hours.
4. While the chicken bakes, heat the demi-glacé. Serve the warmed sauce over the chicken.

Rosemary Chicken Thighs and Legs with Potatoes

 Serves 6

$ Total Cost: $4.60

Calories per Serving: 323

Fat: 8.7 grams

Protein: 28 grams

Sodium: 312.5 mg

Carbohydrates: 33.4 grams

Cholesterol: 104.7 mg

2 pounds chicken thighs and legs

1 leek

8 cloves garlic

6 sprigs rosemary

6 small red potatoes

1 tablespoon olive oil

Fresh-cracked black pepper, to taste

¼ cup capers

1. Preheat oven to 375°F.
2. Remove the skin from the chicken. Slice the leek and mince the garlic. Remove the top 2-inch portion of each rosemary sprig for garnish, and remove the needles from the rest of the rosemary sprigs.
3. Toss all the ingredients except the capers in a baking dish; roast for 1 hour or until the juices run clear from the chicken. Season with pepper and sprinkle with capers.

Sicilian Chicken

Serves 4

 Total Cost: $5.78

 Calories per Serving: 219

Fat: 8.3 grams

Protein: 27 grams

Sodium: 227.2 mg

Carbohydrates: 8.8 grams

Cholesterol: 65.1 mg

4 skinless, boneless chicken breast halves

¼ teaspoon salt

Fresh-cracked black pepper, to taste

4 tablespoons olive oil, divided

½ cup bell pepper strips, assorted colors (about ¼-inch strips)

1 cup thinly sliced red onion

2 garlic cloves, minced

¼ cup chopped fresh basil

2 tablespoons balsamic vinegar

¼–½ teaspoon red pepper flakes

1. Rinse the chicken under cold, running water and pat dry with paper towels. Season with salt and pepper.
2. Heat 2 tablespoons of the oil in a medium-sized nonstick skillet over medium-high heat. Cook the chicken until golden brown, about 4 to 5 minutes per side. Transfer the chicken to a plate and tent with tinfoil to keep warm.
3. Add the remaining oil, peppers, and onions to the skillet; sauté until soft, about 4 minutes, stirring frequently. Add the garlic and sauté for about 1 minute, stirring frequently. Add half of the basil, the vinegar, and red pepper flakes; stir to combine.
4. Add the chicken and any accumulated juices. Cover and reduce heat to medium. Simmer until the chicken is cooked through, about 4 to 6 minutes. Taste and adjust seasoning as desired. Serve hot, garnished with the remaining basil.

Turkey Shish Kabob

 Serves 6

$ Total Cost: $6.68

Calories per Serving: 158

Fat: 6.1 grams

Protein: 14.9 grams

Sodium: 73.9 mg

Carbohydrates: 11.9 grams

Cholesterol: 32.1 mg

1 pound turkey breast
tenderloins

⅓ cup bottled chili sauce

2 tablespoons lemon juice

1 tablespoon sugar

8 mushrooms

8 cherry tomatoes

1 medium zucchini, cut into
½-inch-thick slices

½ green bell pepper, cut into
½-inch squares

2 onions, quartered

2 tablespoons olive oil

1. Cut the turkey tenderloins into 1½-inch cubes and place in a bowl. In a small bowl, stir together the chili sauce, lemon juice, and sugar. Pour over the turkey cubes. Toss to coat. Cover and refrigerate for at least 4 hours or as long as overnight, stirring occasionally.
2. Prepare a fire in a charcoal grill. Remove the turkey from the marinade. Thread the turkey onto skewers alternately with the mushrooms, cherry tomatoes, zucchini, bell pepper, and onions. Brush lightly with the oil and place on the grill rack about 6 inches above medium-hot coals. Grill, turning as needed, and basting occasionally with the marinade, until the turkey is cooked through and the vegetables are tender, about 10 minutes. (Alternatively, cook in a preheated broiler about 6 inches from the heat source for the same amount of time.) Serve hot.

Chicken with Couscous

 Serves 4

$ Total Cost: $3.03

Calories per Serving: 342

Fat: 1.3 grams

Protein: 15.1 grams

Sodium: 203.4 mg

Carbohydrates: 66.6 grams

Cholesterol: 10.5 mg

1 box (8 ounces) instant couscous

½ teaspoon ground cinnamon

½ cup diced cooked chicken breast

1 8-ounce can garbanzo beans, drained and rinsed

¼ cup raisins

⅓ cup low-fat plain yogurt

This satisfying dish is a perfect way to use leftover cooked chicken breast.

1. Cook the couscous according to package directions, adding the cinnamon at the start of cooking. Remove from heat and place in a serving bowl. Stir in the chicken, garbanzos, raisins, and yogurt. Serve immediately.

Garlicky Grilled Chicken

 Serves: 8

 Total Cost: $4.51

Calories per Serving: 269

Fat: 15.2 grams

Protein: 27.1 grams

Sodium: 85.9 mg

Carbohydrates: 6.5 grams

Cholesterol: 65.7 mg

10 cloves garlic, peeled and chopped

3 tablespoons dried oregano, crumbled

1 large red onion, chopped

½ cup olive oil

Salt and pepper to taste

1 cup reduced-sodium, fat-free chicken broth

8 skinless, boneless chicken breast halves

1. In a large shallow dish, combine the garlic, oregano, onion, oil, salt, pepper, and broth. Mix well. Add the chicken, turn to coat well, cover, and marinate in the refrigerator overnight.
2. Prepare a fire in a charcoal grill. Remove the chicken from the marinade and place on the grill rack.
3. Grill, turning once, until tender and the juices run clear when a piece is pierced, about 10 minutes on each side. Serve hot or at room temperature.

Sage-Ricotta Chicken Breasts

 Serves 6

 Total Cost: $4.58

 Calories per Serving: 254

Fat: 10.7 grams

Protein: 28.5 grams

Sodium: 159.8 mg

Carbohydrates: 1.4 grams

Cholesterol: 98.9 mg

6 chicken breast halves with
bone in and skin on

6 fresh sage leaves

½ cup part-skim ricotta cheese

1 egg white

¼ cup niçoise olives

Fresh-cracked black pepper,
to taste

1. Preheat oven to 375°F.
2. Rinse the chicken in cold water. Using your finger, make an opening in the skin where the wing was joined to the breast and loosen the skin away from the breast. Slice the sage.
3. Mix together the sage, cheese, and egg white, and place this mixture in a pastry bag. Pipe the mixture under the skin through the opening you made. Place the chicken on a rack in a baking dish; roast for approximately 30 to 45 minutes, until the internal temperature of the chicken reaches 165°F and the outside is browned.
4. Remove pits and chop olives. After you remove the chicken from the rack, sprinkle with olives and pepper, and serve.

Basting

Meat can be basted in its own drippings, with broth, or with a flavorful sauce both before and during cooking. When you roast meat, you can baste it using a long-handled large spoon, a bulb-type baster, or a basting brush.

Turkey Tetrazzini

 Serves 6

1 pound boneless, skinless
  turkey

1 leek (white part only)

3 cloves garlic

3 cups mushrooms

¼ cup olive oil

⅛ cup bread crumbs

¼ cup all-purpose flour

1 cup skim milk

4 ounces Parmesan cheese,
  grated

Fresh-cracked black pepper,
  to taste

This is best when served over pasta, noodles, or in a
puff pastry shell.

1. Preheat oven to 375°F.
2. Cut the turkey into bite-size portions. Slice the leek and mince
   the garlic. Clean the mushrooms with a damp paper towel,
   then slice them. Mix half of the oil with the bread crumbs.
3. Heat the remaining oil to medium temperature in a medium-
   size saucepan; brown the turkey, then remove and keep
   warm. Add the leeks, garlic, and mushrooms to the pan that
   you cooked the turkey in; cook thoroughly, then slowly stir
   in the flour.
4. Whisk in the milk, stirring constantly to prevent lumping.
   Remove from heat and add turkey and cheese. Spoon the mixture into a casserole pan and top with bread crumb mixture;
   bake for 30 minutes. Season with pepper before serving.

Classic Chicken Parmesan

 Serves 6

Total Cost: $4.93

Calories per Serving: 317

Fat: 14.1 grams

Protein: 37.8 grams

Sodium: 471.8 mg

Carbohydrates: 9 grams

Cholesterol: 123.5 mg

6 boneless, skinless chicken breast halves

1 egg

½ cup bread crumbs

½ teaspoon dried basil

½ teaspoon dried oregano

2 teaspoons minced garlic

2 tablespoons olive oil

1¾ cups Long-Cooking Traditional Tomato Sauce (see recipe in Chapter 5)

½ cup shredded mozzarella cheese

2 tablespoons grated Parmesan cheese

¼ cup chopped fresh parsley

1. Pound the chicken to desired thickness. Beat the egg slightly. Combine the bread crumbs, basil, oregano, and garlic. Dip the chicken in the egg, then into the bread crumb mixture to coat.
2. Heat the oil in an oven-safe pan and sauté the chicken until brown on both sides. Add the tomato sauce, and reduce heat. Cover and simmer for 10 minutes.
3. Preheat broiler. Sprinkle cheeses over the chicken, then place under broiler until cheese is melted. Garnish with parsley before serving.

Roast Chicken

 Serves 6

Total Cost: $4.46

Calories per Serving: 244

Fat: 14.9 grams

Protein: 28.4 grams

Sodium: 422.8 mg

Carbohydrates: 1.1 grams

Cholesterol: 99.3 mg

2 (3-pound) frying chickens

1 teaspoon salt

1 teaspoon pepper

4 cloves garlic, crushed and
   peeled

3 tablespoons olive oil

Juice of 2–3 lemons

½ cup water

1. Preheat oven to 425°F.
2. Rub the chickens with salt, pepper, and crushed garlic. Place in a large roasting pan, breast side up. Brush all over with the oil.
3. Roast for 20 minutes, then reduce heat to 325°F and continue roasting for 50 to 60 minutes.
4. To test doneness, twist a leg joint. If it moves easily, it is done. Pour the lemon juice over the chicken and transfer to platter; keep warm.
5. To make the gravy, add the water to the pan and bring to a boil, stirring constantly until reduced by half. Slice the chicken and serve with gravy.

The $7 a Meal Mediterranean Cookbook

Chicken and Pepper Kabobs

Serves 4

$ Total Cost: $6.88

Calories per Serving: 173

Fat: 5.2 grams

Protein: 17.1 grams

Sodium: 53.4 mg

Carbohydrates: 8.4 grams

Cholesterol: 40.1 mg

1 cup dry red wine

2 tablespoons olive oil

1 teaspoon oregano

1 teaspoon marjoram

1 tablespoon garlic powder

Fresh-cracked black pepper,
   to taste

1 pound boneless, skinless
   chicken breast

4 green Italian peppers

1 red onion

1. Soak 12 wooden skewers in water for 4 hours.
2. Mix together the wine, oil, oregano, marjoram, garlic powder, and black pepper. Marinate the chicken in this mixture
   for approximately 1 hour.
3. Preheat grill.
4. Cut the chicken into 2-inch cubes. Stem, seed, and quarter
   the peppers. Cut the onion into wedges.
5. Thread the chicken, peppers, and onion (alternating them)
   onto the skewers and place them on the grill for approximately 2 minutes on all 4 sides.

Chicken with Rice

Serves 6

Total Cost: $4.23

Calories per Serving: 398

Fat: 13.6 grams

Protein: 13.6 grams

Sodium: 158.7 mg

Carbohydrates: 55.6 grams

Cholesterol: 20.7 mg

3 boneless, skinless chicken breasts, cubed

½ cup olive oil

1 large onion, diced

1 cup diced green bell pepper

½ cup diced red bell pepper

½ cup diced yellow bell pepper

5 cloves garlic, minced

1 tablespoon turmeric

3 cups white long-grain rice, uncooked

4 cups Chicken Stock (see recipe in Chapter 7)

¾ cup chopped green olives

2 bay leaves

Salt and pepper to taste

1. Brown chicken in the oil in a large pot. Remove chicken and set aside.
2. Add onion, peppers, garlic, and turmeric to the pot, and sauté until onions are translucent.
3. Add rice and cook for 5 minutes, stirring occasionally. Add chicken stock, browned chicken, olives, and bay leaves. Stir to combine, bring mixture to a simmer over medium heat, and cover pot with a lid.
4. Simmer 20 minutes or until rice is cooked.
5. Remove bay leaves. Season with salt and pepper.

Chicken Saltimbocca

 Serves 4

 Total Cost: $5.04

 Calories per Serving: 262

Fat: 14.8 grams

Protein: 31.6 grams

Sodium: 433.4 mg

Carbohydrates: 0.2 grams

Cholesterol: 93.6 mg

4 boneless, skinless chicken breasts

Salt and pepper

4 fresh sage leaves

4 slices prosciutto or thinly sliced ham

2 tablespoons butter

2 tablespoons olive oil

1. Pound the chicken breasts flat so they are the same thickness throughout.
2. Season chicken with salt and pepper.
3. Lay one sage leaf on each chicken breast and skewer one slice of prosciutto on top of the sage leaf, covering the whole chicken breast.
4. Heat butter and oil in skillet.
5. Lay chicken in the skillet prosciutto-side down and sauté until crisp. Turn over and finish cooking on the other side.

Lime-Sauced Chicken

 Serves 4

 Total Cost: $3.76

Calories per Serving: 149

Fat: 1.6 grams

Protein: 26.1 grams

Sodium: 123.1 mg

Carbohydrates: 6.9 grams

Cholesterol: 65.1 mg

4 skinless, boneless chicken
   breast halves

½ medium lime

¾ cup apple juice or cider

2 teaspoons cornstarch

½ teaspoon chicken bouillon
   granules

1. Spray a large skillet with nonstick cooking spray and heat over medium heat. Add the chicken and cook, turning to brown evenly, until tender and the juices run clear when a piece is pierced, 8 to 10 minutes. Remove from the skillet and keep warm.
2. Meanwhile, using a vegetable peeler, remove strips of zest from the lime half. Cut zest into narrow strips; set aside. Squeeze 1 tablespoon juice from the lime half. Combine the lime juice, apple juice, cornstarch, and bouillon granules in a bowl, stirring well. Add to the skillet and cook and stir over medium heat until thickened and bubbly, about 10 minutes. Cook and stir for 2 minutes longer. To serve, cut each chicken breast half on the diagonal into 1-inch pieces. Spoon some of the sauce over each serving. Garnish with the reserved lime zest. Pass the remaining sauce.

Chicken and Oregano Risotto

Serves 10

$ Total Cost: $4.30

Calories per Serving: 345

Fat: 10.1 grams

Protein: 27.4 grams

Sodium: 209.8 mg

Carbohydrates: 31.2 grams

Cholesterol: 103.3 mg

2½ pounds skinless, boneless chicken breast

2 large yellow onions

6 cloves garlic

½ cup fresh oregano

2 tablespoons olive oil

1½ cups arborio rice

1 cup dry white wine (not cooking wine)

4½ cups Chicken Stock (see recipe in Chapter 7)

½ cup fresh-grated Asiago cheese

Fresh-cracked black pepper, to taste

1. Cut the chicken into cubes. Peel and finely dice the onions. Peel and mince the garlic. Clean and chop the oregano leaves.
2. Heat the oil to medium-high temperature in a large saucepan. Add the chicken, and cook 5 to 8 minutes, until lightly browned. Add the onions, and sauté for 2 minutes. Add the garlic, and sauté for 1 minute. Add the rice and cook for 1 minute longer, stirring to thoroughly combine the ingredients.
3. Pour in the wine, and stir until completely absorbed. Add the stock ½ cup at a time, stirring frequently and allowing each addition to be completely absorbed before adding the next. Continue until all the stock is absorbed and the rice is tender.
4. Remove from heat, and stir in the cheese, pepper, and oregano. Serve hot.

Turkey and Walnut Risotto

 Serves 10

 Total Cost: $7.00

Calories per Serving: 362

Fat: 13.9 grams

Protein: 22 grams

Sodium: 183.2 mg

Carbohydrates: 33.9 grams

Cholesterol: 68.1 mg

3 tablespoons olive oil

2 pounds boneless turkey (breast, thigh, leg)

¾ cup shelled walnuts

½ bulb fresh garlic

½ cup fresh parsley

1 egg

Kosher salt and fresh-cracked black pepper, to taste

1½ cups arborio rice

¾ cup pinot grigio (or other white drinking wine of choice)

4 cups Chicken Stock (see recipe in Chapter 7)

½ cup fresh-grated Romano cheese

1 tablespoon cold unsalted butter

1. Preheat oven to 375°F. Lightly grease a baking pan with 1 tablespoon of the oil. Clean and dry the turkey, and cut into medallions about ¾ to 1 inch thick. Finely chop or grind the walnuts. Peel and mince the garlic. Clean and gently chop the parsley. Lightly beat the egg.

2. Season the turkey with salt and pepper. Dip turkey in the egg, and then lightly coat with nuts. Heat 1 tablespoon of the oil in a large frying pan. Lightly brown the turkey on each side, about 3 minutes per side. Transfer the turkey to the prepared baking pan. Bake for about 8 to 12 minutes, until cooked through.

3. Add remaining 1 tablespoon of oil to the frying pan and heat to medium temperature. Add garlic and rice, and stir for 1 minute. Pour in wine, and stir until completely absorbed. Add stock ½ cup at a time, stirring frequently and allowing each addition to be completely absorbed before adding the next. Continue until all the stock is absorbed and rice is tender.

4. Remove from heat, and add the turkey, parsley, cheese, and butter. Serve hot.

The $7 a Meal Mediterranean Cookbook

Tuna Casserole

 Serves 6

$ Total Cost: $6.54

Calories per Serving: 439

Fat: 15.8 grams

Protein: 31.8 grams

Sodium: 170.5 mg

Carbohydrates: 40.1 grams

Cholesterol: 48.8 mg

4 cans (6 ounces each) tuna in water, without salt, drained

2 red onions

3 cloves garlic

3 pimientos (fresh or canned)

3 medium potatoes

6 tablespoons olive oil

1 8-ounce can crushed tomatoes

½ teaspoon cayenne pepper

2 tablespoons fresh parsley, chopped

2 bay leaves

½ cup dry white wine

1 cup Fish Stock (see recipe in Chapter 7)

Salt, to taste

Fresh-cracked black pepper, to taste

1. Preheat oven to 350°F.
2. Cut the tuna into cubes. Chop the onions and mince the garlic. Cut the pimientos into strips. Cube the potatoes.
3. Heat the oil in a medium-size sauté pan; sauté the onions and garlic until tender.
4. Add the tuna, and lightly brown. Add the tomatoes, pimientos, cayenne, parsley, and bay leaves. Immediately add the wine, stock, and potatoes. Transfer to a casserole dish and bake, covered, for approximately 1 hour. Remove the bay leaves and season with salt and pepper before serving.

Spicy Shrimp with Lemon Yogurt on Wilted Greens

 Serves 6

$ Total Cost: $5.62

Calories per Serving: 58

Fat: 1.7 grams

Protein: 4.8 grams

Sodium: 105.4 mg

Carbohydrates: 5.2 grams

Cholesterol: 21.8 mg

1 cup nonfat plain yogurt

¼ cup fresh lemon zest

6 cups bitter greens (collard, kale, etc.)

12 large peeled shrimp, tails on

1 teaspoon olive oil

2 cloves garlic, minced

Fresh-cracked black pepper, to taste

¼ cup thinly sliced black olives

1 lemon, cut into wafer-thin slices

1. Prepare the yogurt the night before by mixing together the yogurt and zest, then cover and refrigerate overnight.
2. Wilt the sliced greens in a steamer, then chill immediately (this can be done the night before).
3. Butterfly the shrimp by cutting them down the center, almost but not completely through, and then pushing down the halves to form a butterfly shape. Place the shrimp in a bowl and coat with the oil, garlic, and pepper. Grill or broil until just done (when they've turned white and pink and are firm to the touch).
4. Place the greens in mounds on serving plates, then add the shrimp. Dollop lemon yogurt on top of the shrimp. Sprinkle with the olives and garnish with the lemon slices.

Mushrooms Stuffed with Creamy Crab

 Yields about 11 servings (4 mushrooms/serving)

$ Total Cost: $5.96

Calories per Serving: 61

Fat: 1.6 grams

Protein: 5.5 grams

Sodium: 266.9 mg

Carbohydrates: 7.5 grams

Cholesterol: 5.1 mg

1 tablespoon olive oil

1 clove garlic, minced

2 tablespoons red pepper, diced

1 tablespoon yellow onion, diced

2½ pounds button mushrooms

1 10-ounce can crabmeat

1 egg white

1 tablespoon nonfat plain yogurt

Fresh-cracked black pepper, to taste

Salt, to taste

1 large sprig fresh sage, chopped

1. Preheat oven to 350°F. Spray a baking sheet with cooking spray.
2. Heat the oil in a sauté pan over medium heat. Sauté the garlic, red peppers, and onions until tender.
3. Clean the mushrooms and remove the stems from the caps. Finely chop the stems; set the whole caps aside.
4. Combine the vegetable mixture, chopped stems, crabmeat, egg white, yogurt, pepper, salt, and sage.
5. Stuff the mushroom caps with the crab mixture and arrange on the prepared sheet pan; bake for about 15 minutes.

Basil Creamed Crab

 Serves 6

$ Total Cost: $7.00

Calories per Serving: 218

Fat: 11.8 grams

Protein: 9.3 grams

Sodium: 461.75 mg

Carbohydrates: 18.5 grams

Cholesterol: 33.5 mg

1 4-ounce can crabmeat

8 large basil leaves

Fresh-cracked black pepper,
   to taste

2 cups low-fat sour cream

2 (8- or 9-inch) flour tortillas

1. Preheat oven to 375°F.
2. Flake the crabmeat. Finely slice the basil. In a medium-size bowl, mix together the crab, basil, pepper, and sour cream.
3. Spray a pie pan with cooking spray and place 1 tortilla on the bottom of it. Spoon in the crab mixture, top with the second tortilla, then spray with more cooking spray.
4. Bake for 20 minutes. Let stand 5 minutes, then slice and serve.

Crab and Spinach Risotto

Serves 4

$ Total Cost: $6.28

Calories per Serving: 329

Fat: 9.18 grams

Protein: 12.84 grams

Sodium: 630.31 mg

Carbohydrates: 49.58 grams

Cholesterol: 25.06 mg

1 tablespoon olive oil

1 tablespoon butter

1 onion, finely chopped

3 cloves garlic, minced

2 cups long-grain brown rice

3 cups Chicken Stock (see recipe in Chapter 7)

½ teaspoon salt

⅛ teaspoon pepper

1 cup frozen chopped spinach, thawed

12 ounces flaked surimi

½ cup grated Parmesan cheese

½ cup grated Muenster cheese

Here's a shocker: you can make risotto with regular long-grain rice. You don't need to buy that expensive arborio rice.

1. In large saucepan, combine olive oil and butter. Cook onion and garlic until crisp, about 4 minutes. Stir in rice; cook for 2 minutes longer.
2. Place rice mixture in 3-quart slow cooker. Add stock, salt, and pepper. Cover and cook on low for 6 to 7 hours or until rice is almost tender.
3. Stir in spinach and surimi. Cover and cook on high for 20 to 30 minutes or until hot. Add cheese, cover, and turn off heat. Let stand for 10 minutes, then stir and serve.

Surimi

Surimi, also known as artificial crab, is made of real seafood. Pollock is flavored and colored and shaped to resemble crab legs. It does taste remarkably like the real thing, flakes into small pieces too, and is much less expensive than lump crab. Add it at the very end of any recipe so it doesn't overcook.

Seafood Wontons in Fish Broth

 Serves 6

$ Total Cost: $6.56

Calories per Serving: 251

Fat: 1.5 grams

Protein: 12.1 grams

Sodium: 968.3 mg

Carbohydrates: 42.8 grams

Cholesterol: 30.7 mg

¼ pound crabmeat (fresh or canned)

6 large shrimp

6 sea scallops

1 bunch scallions

6 cloves garlic

1 tablespoon fresh ginger

12 premade wonton skins

½ cup dry white wine or rice wine

Juice of 1 lemon

1 cup Fish Stock (see recipe in Chapter 7)

2 tablespoons soy sauce

1. Chop the crab meat. Clean, peel, devein, and slice the shrimp lengthwise. Slice the scallops into thin coins. Thinly slice the scallions. Mince the garlic and ginger.
2. Mix the seafood with half of the scallions, garlic, and ginger. Spoon the seafood mixture into each wonton skin, fold in half, and seal with fork.
3. In a medium-size, shallow saucepan, combine the remaining garlic and ginger, the wine, juice, stock, and soy sauce; bring to a simmer. Add the wontons and gently simmer for approximately 2 minutes.
4. Serve with the broth, and garnish with remaining scallions.

Shrimp in Filo

Serves 6

1 pound shrimp

½ teaspoon cumin

½ teaspoon garlic powder

¼ teaspoon ground coriander

Fresh-cracked black pepper, to taste

¼ cup cilantro

6 sheets filo dough

2 tablespoons olive oil

½ cup Béchamel (see recipe in Chapter 5)

1. Preheat oven to 375°F.
2. Peel and devein shrimp and remove tails. (You can reserve shells for future stock use.) In a bowl, toss the shrimp with the cumin, garlic powder, coriander, and pepper. Chop the cilantro.
3. Brush both sides of each sheet of filo with the oil. Layer 3 sheets on top of each other, place the shrimp mixture on top, and cover with 3 more layers of filo sheets. Place on a oil-greased baking sheet and bake for 10 to 20 minutes.
4. While shrimp and filo bakes, heat the Béchamel. To serve, slice the shrimp pastries into serving pieces, ladle the sauce over the top, and sprinkle with cilantro.

Orange Shrimp

Serves 10

Total Cost: $6.80

Calories per Serving: 138

Fat: 4.3 grams

Protein: 18.7 grams

Sodium: 143.4 mg

Carbohydrates: 5 grams

Cholesterol: 137.8 mg

2 pounds large shrimp

3 oranges

2 shallots

Fresh-cracked black pepper

1 teaspoon capers, rinsed

2 tablespoons olive oil

1. Peel and devein the shrimp, but leave the tails on. Zest and juice the oranges. Peel and mince the shallots.
2. Mix together the orange juice, zest, shallots, pepper, capers, and oil.
3. Heat the oil mixture in a pan over medium-high temperature.
4. Quickly cook the shrimp in the oil mixture for about 2 or 3 minutes, until opaque in the center.
5. Remove the shrimp from the oil mixture and serve on a platter with a toothpick in each.

Vermicelli with Tuna, Anchovies, and Capers

Serves: 6

Total Cost: $5.98

Calories per Serving: 466

Fat: 11.8 grams

Protein: 20.7 grams

Sodium: 301.7 mg

Carbohydrates: 69.3 grams

Cholesterol: 26 mg

2 tablespoons olive oil

½ cup chopped onion

1 clove garlic, minced

1 16-ounces can plum tomatoes, drained

1 anchovy fillet, finely chopped

2 tablespoons butter, softened

1 pound vermicelli

3 tablespoons capers

1 6½-ounce can water-packed tuna, drained and flaked

2 tablespoons fresh parsley, chopped

1. In a large, deep skillet, heat the oil over medium heat. Add onion and sauté until soft, about 5 to 7 minutes. Add the garlic and sauté briefly. Add the tomatoes, break them up with a wooden spoon, cover, and simmer until soft, about 10 minutes.
2. Place the chopped anchovy in a small bowl and mash with a spoon. (Alternatively, process in a mini food processor.) Add the butter to the anchovy and mash together with a fork.
3. Meanwhile, cook the pasta in boiling salted water until al dente. Scoop out ½ cup of the cooking water. Drain the pasta.
4. Stir enough of the reserved cooking water into the anchovy butter to make it thick and smooth and no longer a paste. Add the capers to the skillet and stir to blend. Add the tuna and heat through over medium heat. Add the pasta to the sauce and toss until the pasta is coated. Transfer to a warmed bowl, sprinkle with the parsley, and serve.

CHAPTER 14

BEEF, PORK, VEAL, AND LAMB

Stuffed Artichokes

 Serves 6

3 artichokes

1 medium yellow onion

1 shallot

4 cloves garlic

6 slices Italian bread

1 pound lean ground beef

1 egg

4 sprigs oregano, chopped

2 sprigs basil, chopped

Fresh-cracked black pepper, to taste

2 ounces Parmesan cheese, grated

1. Preheat oven to 375°F.
2. Cut the artichokes in half lengthwise. Leave the stems on but peel them with a vegetable peeler. Remove and discard the chokes (the prickly white and purple center). Blanch the artichoke halves for 20 to 40 minutes or until the artichokes are tender, then immediately shock them in an ice-water bath.
3. Dice the onion and shallot. Mince the garlic. Soak the bread slices in water, then squeeze out the water.
4. Coat a deep roasting pan with cooking spray. Mix together the ground beef, egg, bread, onions, shallots, garlic, oregano, basil, pepper, and Parmesan cheese. Stuff the mixture between the artichoke leaves and place cut-side down in the pan.
5. Bake, covered, for 45 minutes. Uncover and bake for another 10 to 15 minutes.

Apricot-Stuffed Pork Tenderloin

Serves 6

$ Total Cost: $7.00

Calories per Serving: 253

Fat: 10.9 grams

Protein: 29 grams

Sodium: 347.6 mg

Carbohydrates: 11.9 grams

Cholesterol: 72.4 mg

1¼-pound pork tenderloin

1 shallot

3 cloves garlic

½ cup dried apricots

¼ cup pecans

3 fresh sage leaves

Fresh-cracked black pepper, to taste

Kosher salt, to taste

1. Preheat oven to 375°F.
2. Butterfly the tenderloin by making a lengthwise slice down the middle, making certain not to cut completely through.
3. Mince the shallot and garlic. Remove pits and slice apricots. Chop the pecans and sage.
4. Lay out the tenderloin. Layer all ingredients over the tenderloin and season with pepper and salt. Carefully roll up the loin and tie securely.
5. Spray a rack with cooking spray, then place the tenderloin on the rack and roast for 1 to 1½ hours. Let cool slightly, then slice.

Beef Braciola

Serves 6

 Total Cost: $6.48

 Calories per Serving: 408

Fat: 28.2 grams

Protein: 28.4 grams

Sodium: 452.9 mg

Carbohydrates: 4.7 grams

Cholesterol: 125.4 mg

1 small yellow onion

1 shallot

4 cloves garlic

¼ cup fresh parsley

1 hard-boiled egg

3 thin slices provolone cheese

3 thin slices ham

6 black olives

1 pound beef tenderloin

Fresh-cracked black pepper, to taste

1 teaspoon olive oil

½ cup dry red wine

2 cups Long-Cooking Traditional Tomato Sauce (see recipe in Chapter 5)

1 cup brown Demi-Glacé Reduction Sauce (see recipe in Chapter 5)

1. Small-dice the onion and shallot. Mince the garlic and parsley. Peel and chop the egg. Finely dice the cheese and ham. Chop the olives.
2. Lay out the beef and layer the onion, shallot, garlic, parsley, egg, cheese, ham, olives, and pepper on top. Roll up and tie each end closed.
3. Hcat the oil to medium-high temperature. Sear the braciola on all sides, then add the wine and let reduce by half. Reduce temperature to medium-low. Add the sauces and simmer on low heat for 3 hours.
4. To serve, untie the braciola and serve with pasta.

Breaded Pork Chops

 Serves 6

 Total Cost: $6.97

Calories per Serving: 198

Fat: 4.9 grams

Protein: 26.2 grams

Sodium: 484.1 mg

Carbohydrates: 12.6 grams

Cholesterol: 64.3 mg

3 slices pumpernickel bread

6 cloves garlic

½ cup applesauce

1 teaspoon olive oil

6 pork chops

Fresh-cracked black pepper,
to taste

Kosher salt, to taste

1. Preheat oven to 375°F. Spray a baking sheet with cooking spray.
2. Toast the bread and grate into crumbs. Mince the garlic in a blender, then add the applesauce and oil, and blend until smooth.
3. Rub the chops with the garlic-applesauce mixture. Bread with pumpernickel crumbs and place on prepared baking sheet. Spray the chops with cooking spray and season with pepper and salt.
4. Bake for 20 minutes, then turn and bake for 20 to 40 minutes longer, depending on the thickness of the pork. Serve hot.

Grilled Rack of Lamb

Serves 6

Total Cost: $5.29
Calories per Serving: 307
Fat: 19.6 grams
Protein: 29.8 grams
Sodium: 96.8 mg
Carbohydrates: 0.8 grams
Cholesterol: 99.9 mg

6 racks of lamb (4 chop portions)
2 tablespoons olive oil
Kosher salt, to taste
Fresh-cracked black pepper, to taste

1 cup brown Demi-Glacé Reduction Sauce (see recipe in Chapter 5)

1. Preheat grill.
2. Brush the lamb with the oil and season with salt and pepper. Place lamb on grill and cook to desired doneness.
3. While the meat cooks, heat the demi-glacé. Ladle the sauce on serving plates. Slice the chops and fan over sauce to serve.

Lamb Samosas

Serves 6

½ cup whole-wheat flour

½ cup all-purpose flour

2 tablespoons curry powder

1 teaspoon ground cumin

¼ teaspoon ground coriander

¼ cup plus 1 teaspoon olive oil

½ cup water

1 shallot

4 cloves garlic

1 pound ground lamb

Fresh-crushed black pepper, to taste

4 sprigs mint, leaves only

1. To prepare the dough: Sift together the flours and half the amounts of curry, cumin, and coriander. Mix ¼ cup of the oil with the water. Mix together the wet and dry ingredients with dough hook on low speed (or by hand). Allow the dough to rest for 1 hour in the refrigerator.
2. Near the end of the resting period, preheat oven to 350°F.
3. Mince the shallot and garlic. Heat the remaining oil to medium temperature in a large sauté pan; sauté the lamb, garlic, and shallots with black pepper and the remainder of the curry, cumin, and coriander until the meat begins to brown. Remove and let cool.
4. Roll out the dough to ¼-inch thickness on a floured surface, and cut into 4-inch circles. Place the lamb mixture in the centers of the circles, top with mint, then fold and seal edges closed; bake for 10 to 15 minutes, until the dough is brown.

What Are Samosas?

Samosas are an East Indian savory "turnover." You can often find vendors on the streets in India selling these as snacks.

Meat Loaf

 Serves 6

$ Total Cost: $6.94

Calories per Serving: 382

Fat: 16.4 grams

Protein: 30.5 grams

Sodium: 515.9 mg

Carbohydrates: 27.4 grams

Cholesterol: 115 mg

4 slices toasted Italian bread

2 plum tomatoes

1 yellow onion

6 cloves garlic

¼ cup fresh parsley

2 sprigs fresh thyme

6 green olives

6 black olives

3 thin slices Swiss cheese

1 pound lean ground beef

1 egg, beaten

1 tablespoon honey

Fresh-cracked black pepper, to taste

Pinch of kosher salt, to taste

1. Preheat oven to 375°F.
2. Soak the toast in water for 30 seconds, then squeeze out liquid. Chop the tomatoes; dice the onion; mince the garlic, parsley, and thyme; chop the olives; and finely dice the cheese.
3. Mix together all the ingredients and form into desired shape. Roast for 45 to 60 minutes, until the internal temperature reaches 170°F. Slice and serve.

Pork Casserole

 Serves 6

$ Total Cost: $6.95

Calories per Serving: 159

Fat: 2.7 grams

Protein: 17.5 grams

Sodium: 205.7 mg

Carbohydrates: 17.3 grams

Cholesterol: 42.9 mg

1 apple

1 pear

2 yellow onions

1 stalk celery

1 fennel bulb

½ small head cabbage

1 tablespoon olive oil

1 pound pork

½ teaspoon fennel seeds

½ teaspoon caraway seeds

Fresh-cracked black pepper, to taste

¼ cup red wine vinegar

1 cup apple or other fruit juice

1. Preheat oven to 350°F.
2. Dice the apple, pear, and onions. Slice the celery, fennel, and cabbage.
3. Grease a casserole pan with the olive oil. Alternate layers of pork, fruit, vegetables, seeds, pepper, vinegar, and juice.
4. Bake, covered, for 45 minutes, then uncover and continue baking for 15 minutes longer. Let cool slightly, then cut and serve.

Pork with Poblanos and Prosciutto

 Serves 6

$ Total Cost: $6.38

Calories per Serving: 174

Fat: 9.7 grams

Protein: 20.8 grams

Sodium: 365.5 mg

Carbohydrates: 1.4 grams

Cholesterol: 51.1 mg

2 poblano chili peppers

1 tablespoon olive oil

¼ cup walnuts

1 pound pork tenderloin

4 thin slices prosciutto or ham

1. Preheat oven to 375°F. Spray a cooking rack with cooking spray.
2. Rub the poblanos with half of the oil. Roast for 15 minutes; remove from oven and place in a plastic bag until cool. Then remove the skins and seeds.
3. In a blender or food processor, blend together the walnuts, poblano, and remaining oil until smooth.
4. Rub the poblano mixture onto the tenderloin and wrap the loin with the proscuitto slices; place on rack in a roasting pan. Cover loosely with foil and roast for 1 to 1½ hours. Slice and serve.

Seared Pork Medallions

 Serves 6

Total Cost: $6.70

Calories per Serving: 257.1

Fat: 9.4 grams

Protein: 33.3 grams

Sodium: 434.8 mg

Carbohydrates: 4.3 grams

Cholesterol: 86.1 mg

1¼ pounds boneless pork tenderloin

6 cloves garlic

¼ cup pitted olives

1 tablespoon olive oil

Pinch of kosher salt, to taste

Fresh-cracked black pepper, to taste

½ cup arugula, chopped after measuring

½ cup dry red wine

½ cup Red Wine Vegetable Stock (see recipe in Chapter 7)

1. Thinly slice the pork. Mince the garlic. Slice the olives.
2. Heat a sauté pan to medium-high temperature. Brush the pan with some of the oil. Season the pork with salt and pepper, then sauté on each side for less than a minute. Remove pork from pan and keep warm.
3. Reduce heat to medium and add remainder of oil to pan. Add garlic and arugula; sauté for 2 minutes. Add the wine and let it reduce for 1 minute, then add the stock. Let this cook for at least 10 minutes so the flavors can mingle.
4. Season the arugula mixture with pepper, then place on plates and arrange the pork on top. Sprinkle the olives over the top, and serve.

Stewed Short Ribs of Beef

 Serves 6

 Total Cost: $6.86

 Calories per Serving: 439

Fat: 8.8 grams

Protein: 35.8 grams

Sodium: 201.4 mg

Carbohydrates: 12.2 grams

Cholesterol: 101.3 mg

1 large yellow onion

1¼ pounds short ribs of beef

1 tablespoon ground cumin

Fresh-cracked black pepper, to taste

1 tablespoon olive oil

2 cans (14 ounces each) crushed tomatoes

1 cup dry red wine

1 quart Red Wine Vegetable Stock (Chapter 7)

1. Preheat oven to 325°F.
2. Roughly chop the onion. Season the ribs with cumin and pepper.
3. Heat the oil to medium-high temperature in a Dutch oven, and sear the ribs on all sides. Add the onions and sauté for 2 minutes, then add the tomatoes and sauté 1 minute more. Add the wine and let reduce by half.
4. Add the stock. When stock begins to boil, cover and place in oven for 1 to 1½ hours.
5. Drain ribs and vegetables. Keep warm. Place Dutch oven on top of stove on high heat and let sauce thicken to a gravy-type consistency.

Sautéed Pork Medallions and Potatoes

 Serves 6

Total Cost: $6.51

Calories per Serving: 289

Fat: 4.9 grams

Protein: 25.3 grams

Sodium: 265.9 mg

Carbohydrates: 37 grams

Cholesterol: 57 mg

1¼ pounds pork tenderloin

2 pounds Idaho or russet potatoes

½ cup fresh oregano

½ bulb garlic

2 tablespoons black olives

Fresh-cracked black pepper, to taste

1½ teaspoons olive oil

1. Slice the pork into thin medallions. Slice the potatoes. Chop the oregano. Mince the garlic and olives. Season the pork and potatoes with pepper.
2. Heat the olive oil in a sauté pan over medium heat. Add the pork, then season with half of the oregano and half the garlic.
3. Stir in the potatoes and season with the other half of the oregano and garlic. Turn heat to medium-low; cover and cook for approximately 20 minutes.
4. Flip the potatoes and pork; cook, uncovered, for 10 more minutes. To serve, divide the potatoes and pork among the plates, and sprinkle with olives.

Sausage Patties

 Serves 6

 Total Cost: $4.00

 Calories per Serving: 378

Fat: 30.3 grams

Protein: 23.8 grams

Sodium: 181.1 mg

Carbohydrates: 1.2 grams

Cholesterol: 127 mg

2 ounces pork fat

2 ounces ham

1 pound ground pork

1 egg

1 tablespoon fresh-cracked black pepper, to taste

1 tablespoon dried sage

¼ teaspoon dried red pepper flakes

1 teaspoon ground cumin

Kosher salt, to taste

1 tablespoon olive oil

1. Finely dice the pork fat and ham. Mix together all the ingredients except the oil until thoroughly blended; form into patties.
2. Heat the oil to medium temperature in a skillet. Brown patties for about 7 minutes on each side, covered with a lid to ensure thorough cooking. Drain on paper-toweled rack, then serve.

Marinated London Broil

 Serves 6

$ Total Cost: $5.85

Calories per Serving: 288

Fat: 12.5 grams

Protein: 34.9 grams

Sodium: 126.5 mg

Carbohydrates: 1.6 grams

Cholesterol: 65.8 mg

1 cup dry red wine

1 tablespoon olive oil

1 teaspoon ground cinnamon

½ teaspoon ground cloves

1 teaspoon ground cumin

Fresh-cracked black pepper,
    to taste

Kosher salt, to taste

1½-pound London broil

1. Preheat grill. Mix together the wine, oil, and seasonings in
   a shallow bowl or pan. Coat the London broil in the mixture,
   then grill to desired doneness. Slice on a bias and serve.

Beef and Polenta Casserole

 Serves 10

$ Total Cost: $4.13

Calories per Serving: 272

Fat: 15.7 grams

Protein: 23.8 grams

Sodium: 146 mg

Carbohydrates: 7.9 grams

Cholesterol: 74.1 mg

2 tablespoons olive oil

2 Vidalia onions

1 shallot

1 bulb garlic

4 tomatoes

3 sprigs basil

1½ pounds lean ground beef

½ recipe Polenta (see recipe in Chapter 2)

1 bunch steamed escarole (or any bitter greens)

½ cup ricotta

Fresh-cracked black pepper, to taste (optional)

¼ cup fresh-grated Romano cheese

2 tablespoons melted unsalted butter

1. Preheat oven to 350°F. Lightly grease a large casserole dish with 1 tablespoon of the oil. Peel and dice the onions. Peel and mince the shallot and garlic. Clean and slice the tomatoes. Clean and gently chop the basil leaves.
2. Heat the remaining oil to medium temperature in a skillet. Add the onions, shallots, garlic, and beef. Sauté for 10 to 15 minutes, until the beef is browned. Drain off excess grease.
3. Spread a thin layer of the polenta in the bottom of the prepared casserole dish. Spread layers of the beef, tomatoes, escarole, ricotta, basil, and pepper on top. Top with the remaining polenta. Sprinkle with the cheese. Drizzle with the butter.
4. Bake for 20 minutes, and serve.

CHAPTER 15

FRESH FRUITS AND DESSERTS

Acorn Squash Bake

 Serves 6

 Total Cost: $5.52

 Calories per Serving: 219

Fat: 0.5 grams

Protein: 3.1 grams

Sodium: 11.9 mg

Carbohydrates: 56.4 grams

Cholesterol: 0 mg

3 acorn squashes

2 cups apple juice

6 teaspoons fresh-grated
orange zest

6 teaspoons rolled oats

6 teaspoons raisins

3 teaspoons ground cinnamon

1 teaspoon ground nutmeg

1. Preheat oven to 375°F.
2. Cut the acorn squashes in half and remove seeds. Place halves cut-side down in a small roasting pan. Pour the apple juice over the top and cover tightly.
3. Bake for approximately 40 minutes. Remove from oven and turn squashes cut-side up. Sprinkle each with 1 teaspoon zest, 1 teaspoon oats, 1 teaspoon raisins, ½ teaspoon cinnamon, and a dash of nutmeg.
4. Baste with reduced apple juice in the pan. Cover and bake for 10 minutes longer. Then uncover and bake 10 minutes longer. Serve in individual bowls.

Acorn Squash

Acorn squash has a flavor similar to pumpkin and sweet potato. If you enjoy the taste of those two traditional favorites, you'll love the Acorn Squash Bake.

Date-Almond Tart

Serves 6

$ Total Cost: $4.96	
Calories per Serving: 338	
Fat: 6.2 grams	
Protein: 4.9 grams	
Sodium: 33.1 mg	
Carbohydrates: 68.2 grams	
Cholesterol: 0.8 mg	

1 cup flour

2 teaspoons olive oil

1 teaspoon ice water

1 cup chopped dried dates

½ cup chopped almonds

½ cup honey

1 cup plain nonfat yogurt

¼ cup confectioners' sugar

1. Preheat oven to 375°F.
2. Mix together flour, olive oil, and ice water to form dough. Roll out dough into a 12-inch circle. Place in 9-inch quiche or pie pan.
3. Mix together the dates, almonds, and honey. Place the date mixture in the center of the dough and loosely fold over pastry edges.
4. Bake for 20 minutes. Let cool and serve with yogurt and sprinkled confectioners' sugar.

The $7 a Meal Mediterranean Cookbook

Figs with Brie and Port Wine Reduction

 Serves 6

$ Total Cost: $7.00

Calories per Serving: 312

Fat: 14.6 grams

Protein: 9.4 grams

Sodium: 263.1 mg

Carbohydrates: 27.6 grams

Cholesterol: 49 mg

1 cup port wine

1 tablespoon cold unsalted butter

6 ounces Brie cheese

6 fresh figs

¼ cup confectioners' sugar

1. Heat the wine on medium in a medium-size saucepan, and let reduce by half. Remove from heat and add the cold butter.
2. Cut the Brie into six equal portions. Cut the figs in half.
3. To serve, drizzle wine reduction on plates, sprinkle with confectioners' sugar, and arrange figs and Brie on top.

Fresh Fruit Chowder

Serves 6

$ Total Cost: $4.43

Calories per Serving: 97

Fat: 0.8 grams

Protein: 0.7 grams

Sodium: 12.8 mg

Carbohydrates: 23.4 grams

Cholesterol: 0.2 mg

3 peaches

½ cup strawberries

½ cup blueberries

½ cup blackberries

3 sprigs mint

1 8-ounce can cubed
   pineapple

3 ounces nonfat plain yogurt

¼ cup unsweetened cocoa
   powder (optional)

1. Cut the peaches into wedges. Slice the strawberries. Slice
   the blackberries in half. Remove the bottom leaves from the
   mint sprigs and save the tops for garnish.
2. Purée the pineapple in a blender or food processor
   until smooth.
3. Mix puréed pineapple with other fruit and place in a shallow bowl. Dollop with yogurt and sprinkle with mint leaves
   and cocoa.

Roasted Pears

 Serves 12

 Total Cost: $5.58

 Calories per Serving: 158

Fat: 0.3 grams

Protein: 1.4 grams

Sodium: 13.2 mg

Carbohydrates: 33.3 grams

Cholesterol: 0.7 mg

6 pears

6 sprigs fresh mint

1 cup sweet white wine

1 tablespoon lemon zest

1 teaspoon honey

6 tablespoons low-fat vanilla
yogurt

1. Preheat oven to 375°F.
2. Peel the pears and cut in half from top to bottom. Chop the
   mint, saving the tops for garnish. Place the pears cut-side
   down in a small roasting pan and pour the wine over them.
   Sprinkle with zest and drizzle with honey.
3. Cover tightly and roast for approximately 40 minutes. Then
   uncover and roast for 10 minutes longer.
4. To serve, place 1 tablespoon of yogurt on each plate. Prop
   half a pear on dollop and sprinkle with chopped mint. Place
   mint sprig tops on sides for garnish.

Apricot Pastry

 Serves 6

$ Total Cost: $6.66

Calories per Serving: 360

Fat: 8.3 grams

Protein: 5.7 grams

Sodium: 13.8 mg

Carbohydrates: 71 grams

Cholesterol: 0 mg

1 cup flour

2 teaspoons olive oil

1 teaspoon ice water

2 cups chopped apricots

½ cup chopped walnuts

½ cup currants

¼ cup apricot jam

¼ cup light brown sugar

1. Preheat oven to 375°F.
2. Mix together flour, olive oil, and ice water to form dough. Roll out the dough into a large square and place on baking sheet.
3. Arrange the apricots, nuts, currants, jam, and sugar in the center and pinch together the edges up to 1 or 2 inches from center. Fold back corners to leave small opening in center. Bake for 30 minutes.

Lime Tart

 Serves 6

$ Total Cost: $2.63

Calories per Serving: 314

Fat: 19.3 grams

Protein: 5 grams

Sodium: 38.4 mg

Carbohydrates: 31.4 grams

Cholesterol: 125.6 mg

TART CRUST

¼ cup unsalted butter

¼ cup olive oil

¼ cup whole-wheat flour

½ cup all-purpose flour

1 tablespoon water

LIME FILLING

3 limes

3 eggs, beaten

2 tablespoons cornstarch

½ cup granulated sugar

1 cup water

1. Preheat oven to 375°F.
2. To make the crust: Blend the butter and oil; sift together the flours; then combine the two mixtures with a dough hook at low speed (or by hand), adding the water 1 spoonful at a time until the mixture forms a ball. Roll out the dough to a 12-inch disk on a floured surface and place in a 9-inch pie pan. Bake for 10 minutes; remove from oven.
3. To make the lime filling: Juice the limes and grate the rinds for zest. Mix together all the filling ingredients; bring to a slow simmer in a medium-size saucepan, stirring constantly until it becomes thick. Pour the lime mixture into the pie shell and bake 15 minutes longer.

Poached Apples

Serves 6

$ Total Cost: $2.96

Calories per Serving: 217

Fat: 0.3 grams

Protein: 0.7 grams

Sodium: 4.7 mg

Carbohydrates: 31.6 grams

Cholesterol: 0 mg

6 Granny Smith apples

1 lemon

1 cup cider

¼ cup sweet white wine

3 whole cloves (or ¼ teaspoon ground cloves)

2 cinnamon sticks (or ½ teaspoon ground cinnamon)

¼ cup golden raisins

1. Peel and core the apples. Zest and juice the lemon.
2. Place the apples in a large saucepan with the cider, wine, lemon juice, zest, cloves, and cinnamon; simmer, covered, on medium heat for 30 to 45 minutes, until the apples are fork tender. Remove apples and keep warm.
3. Reduce the cooking liquid and remove the cloves and cinnamon sticks before serving. Spoon reduced liquid over each apple and sprinkle with raisins.

Which White Wine?
If you use a crisp, dry white wine you'll get a less sweet product. Instead, try using a sweet dessert white wine and savor the richness.

Raspberries with Peach Sauce

Serves 4

 Total Cost: $5.42

 Calories per Serving: 101

Fat: 3.1 grams

Protein: 2.7 grams

Sodium: 14 mg

Carbohydrates: 17.3 grams

Cholesterol: 6.6 mg

4 large peaches

2 teaspoons rice wine vinegar

3 teaspoons confectioners' sugar

2 cups fresh raspberries

½ cup crème fraîche

1. Peel and pit the peaches; purée in blender. Add the vinegar and sugar to desired sweetness. Refrigerate until ready to serve. To serve, decorate plate with sauce. Top with equal amounts of raspberries and a dollop of crème fraîche.

Blueberry Ravioli

 Serves 6

½ cup all-purpose flour
¼ cup whole-wheat flour
¼ cup semolina flour
¼ cup granulated sugar
1 whole egg
1 egg white
2 tablespoons olive oil

1 tablespoon water
1 pint blueberries
¼ cup confectioners' sugar
1 teaspoon fresh-grated lemon zest

1. Mix together the flours, granulated sugar, egg, egg white, oil, and water on low speed until fully incorporated. Let dough rest 1 hour in refrigerator.
2. Roll out the dough on a floured surface. Cut into 4-inch squares and put a spoonful of blueberries into each square. Fold to form a triangle, and seal.
3. Bring 2 gallons of water to boil. Cook the ravioli for approximately 6 to 8 minutes. Lift ravioilis out of the water, place on plates, and sprinkle with confectioners' sugar and zest before serving.

Sautéed Strawberries in Yogurt Soup

 Serves 6

1 cup skim milk

1 teaspoon vanilla extract

2 tablespoons granulated sugar

2 cups nonfat plain yogurt

1 pint strawberries

1 tablespoon unsalted butter

¼ cup brown sugar

1. Heat the milk with the vanilla extract and granulated sugar in a small saucepan; let cool. When the milk is completely cooled, whisk in the yogurt.
2. Slice the strawberries. Melt the butter and toss with the strawberries.
3. Serve yogurt soup in shallow bowl. Dollop with strawberry mixture and sprinkle with brown sugar.

Grilled Bananas

 Serves 6

$ Total Cost: $2.67

Calories per Serving: 196

Fat: 3.3 grams

Protein: 2.5 grams

Sodium: 4 mg

Carbohydrates: 43 grams

Cholesterol: 0 mg

¼ cup almonds

1 sprig cilantro (optional)

6 bananas

2 tablespoons honey

¼ cup light brown sugar

You can also grill the bananas unpeeled. Grill until the peel is black, remove, and split the banana. This works great for campfires, too!

1. Preheat grill. Chop the almonds and cilantro.
2. Peel the bananas, spray with cooking spray, and place on grill. Move them during grilling to form an X-shaped grill mark on them.
3. To serve, slice the bananas on bias, fan on plate, drizzle with honey, and sprinkle with almonds, brown sugar, and cilantro.

Types of Bananas

There are hundreds of types of bananas. You are probably most familiar with the yellow Cavendish banana. However, your market may carry other varieties such as the red banana, which is sweeter than the Cavendish, or the Manzano, which has an apple flavor. If you like bananas, try them all!

The $7 a Meal Mediterranean Cookbook

Yogurt Custard

 Serves 6

Total Cost: $6.84

Calories per Serving: 163

Fat: 7.9 grams

Protein: 7 grams

Sodium: 62.6 mg

Carbohydrates: 17.5 mg

Cholesterol: 190.2 mg

6 large egg yolks

3½ cups unsweetened yogurt

4 teaspoons honey

4 cups seasonal berries and
   fruit

1. Over medium heat, stir the yolks, yogurt, and honey until
   thickened and boiled. Let cool slightly. Arrange your choice
   of fruit on a serving plate and top with custard.

Citrus Sherbet

 Serves 8

Total Cost: $3.38

Calories per Serving: 116

Fat: 0.1 grams

Protein: 1.5 grams

Sodium: 60.7 mg

Carbohydrates: 28.6 grams

Cholesterol: 0 mg

4 Valencia oranges

2 Ruby Red grapefruits

1 key lime

1¼ cups granulated sugar

⅓ cup water

3 egg whites

¼ teaspoon salt

¼ teaspoon cream of tartar

Edible orchid or mint leaves, for garnish

1. Juice the oranges, grapefruits, and lime, then measure out 3 cups of unfiltered juice and set aside.
2. In a saucepan, combine the sugar and water. Bring to a boil, stirring until the sugar dissolves. Cook to 238°F (soft ball on a candy thermometer or the sugar forms a soft ball when dropped into cold water).
3. While this is cooking, beat the egg whites with the salt and cream of tartar until stiff. Slowly pour the hot syrup into the mixing bowl with the egg whites, continuing to beat at high speed. Continue to beat until the mixture is stiff and glossy (approximately 5 minutes).
4. Stir in the juices, then pour mixture into a shallow pan. Freeze until almost firm, then return to the bowl. Beat again until blended. Return the sherbet to the container and freeze until ready to serve.
5. To serve: Remove from freezer, allowing 15 minutes before serving. Scoop and garnish.

Fig and Rhubarb Pie

 Serves 12

$ Total Cost: $3.83	
Calories per Serving: 317	
Fat: 11.1 grams	
Protein: 5.1 grams	
Sodium: 79.7 mg	
Carbohydrates: 50.4 grams	
Cholesterol: 55.9 mg	

2½ cups flour

½ cup granulated sugar

⅓ teaspoon salt

1 stick (½ cup) unsalted butter

1 large whole egg

1 egg yolk

Zest of 1 lemon

2½ tablespoons fresh lemon juice

1½ pounds rhubarb, trimmed and cut into chunks

¼ cup confectioners' sugar

¾ cup brown sugar, plus extra for sprinkling

½ cup water

1 teaspoon vanilla

1 cup chopped fresh figs

½ cup slivered almonds

1. To make the dough: Using a dough hook (or food processor) combine the flour, granulated sugar, and salt. Incorporate the butter by cutting it in with a pastry blender. (At this point you should pulse again if using processor to form a ball.) Add the whole egg, yolk, zest, and juice. Combine until dough forms a ball. Wrap in film and chill for 30 minutes.

2. To make the filling: In a saucepan, combine trimmed and chunked rhubarb with the confectioners' and brown sugars and water. Cook over medium heat until the liquid starts to thicken. Remove from heat and stir in the vanilla and figs. Cover and refrigerate for a couple of hours.

3. Preheat oven to 375°F.

4. Evenly divide the dough into two balls. Roll out the first piece on lightly floured surface to fit a 10-inch pie or tart pan. Place rolled-out dough in the pan and fill with the fig-rhubarb mixture. Top evenly with almonds.

5. Roll out the second piece of dough large enough to cover the pan. Cut into ½-inch strips. Make lattice on top of filling. Pinch together with the bottom dough. Remove excess dough around edges with knife.

6. Sprinkle with a small amount of brown sugar and bake 45 minutes or until the top is golden. Cool completely before serving.

Orange Crepes

 Serves 6

$ Total Cost: $1.54

Calories per Serving: 128

Fat: 2.8 grams

Protein: 5.4 grams

Sodium: 50.3 mg

Carbohydrates: 20.2 grams

Cholesterol: 72.3 mg

½ cup flour

2 whole eggs

2 egg whites

½ cup skim milk

1½ cups fresh orange juice

1 teaspoon fresh orange zest

½ teaspoon melted butter

1 teaspoon cold unsalted butter

¼ cup confectioners' sugar

1. In a bowl, mix together the flour, whole eggs, egg whites, milk, ¼ cup of the orange juice, and ½ teaspoon of the orange zest.
2. Heat a griddle or sauté pan to medium temperature. Brush with melted butter and pour in batter. When batter begins to bubble and bottom of crepe is light golden brown, flip over and cook for just a few seconds. Remove and keep warm. Repeat with the remaining batter.
3. Prepare orange syrup by boiling the remaining juice in a small pot. Continue boiling until juice is reduced by half, then add the teaspoon of cold butter.
4. To serve, place each crepe on a plate (fold if desired), drizzle with orange syrup, and sprinkle with remaining zest and the sugar.

Whole Butter

Whole butter contains a mix of fats, milk solids, and water and is typically used for baking and cooking since it has a low smoking point. Cold whole butter serves to slightly thicken sauces. Try it with this recipe to get a thicker orange syrup. Also, use it in other recipes where a thicker sauce appeals to you.

Rice Pudding with Cherries in Wine

 Serves 6

 Total Cost: $4.22

 Calories per Serving: 313

Fat: 3.8 grams

Protein: 5.6 grams

Sodium: 50 mg

Carbohydrates: 57.1 grams

Cholesterol: 11.1 mg

1 cup port wine

¾ cup granulated sugar

1 pint Bing cherries, pitted

1 quart whole milk

1 cup basmati or jasmine rice

1 cinnamon stick

Zest of 1 lemon

4 tablespoons granulated sugar

1. In a saucepan, heat the wine and ¾ cup sugar over medium heat until the sugar dissolves. Add the cherries, and sauté for 2 minutes. Remove cherries and reduce sauce to the consistency of a dry, light jelly (also known as sec). Then mix the cherries back in and let cool.
2. In a pan, combine the milk, rice, cinnamon stick, and zest. Cook about 1 hour at low-medium temperature, stirring frequently.
3. Add the sugar to the milk mixture and stir until dissolved. Remove cinnamon stick, and spoon pudding into serving dishes. Let the pudding cool. When ready to serve, crown with cherries and wine mixture.

Clafoutis with Fruit

Serves 2

Total Cost: $4.52

Calories per Serving: 135

Fat: 3.7 grams

Protein: 3.6 grams

Sodium: 36.7 mg

Carbohydrates: 22.6 grams

Cholesterol: 59.3 mg

2 teaspoons unsalted butter

2 cups seasonal fruit (cherries, raspberries, blueberries, blackberries, etc.)

½ cup granulated sugar

2 eggs

1½ cups milk

6 teaspoons all-purpose flour

Confectioners' sugar

1. Preheat oven to 400°F.
2. Butter two individual ovenproof dishes using ½ teaspoon of butter each. Sprinkle the 2 cups fruit with ¼ cup of the granulated sugar and arrange half of the mixture in the bottom of each dish.
3. Mix together the eggs, milk, remaining butter and granulated sugar, and the flour 1 teaspoon at a time until a smooth batter is formed.
4. Pour half of this mixture over the fruit in each dish and bake for approximately 20 minutes; then reduce heat to 325°F and bake 10 minutes more. Insert a knife in the custard to test doneness. If the custard sticks to the knife, it isn't done yet. When the knife comes out clean, it is done.
5. Sprinkle with confectioners' sugar and serve.

Pistachio Biscotti with Peach Sauce

Serves 8

Total Cost: $3.52

Calories per Serving: 264

Fat: 6 grams

Protein: 6.6 grams

Sodium: 149.6 mg

Carbohydrates: 46.6 grams

Cholesterol: 51.9 mg

2 eggs

1 teaspoon almond extract

1 teaspoon vanilla extract

½ cup granulated sugar

1¾ cups cake flour

1 teaspoon baking powder

¼ teaspoon salt

⅔ cup shelled pistachio nuts

½ cup Peach Sauce (see Raspberries with Peach Sauce recipe in this chapter)

When buying shelled pistachios, make sure the shell is split and partially open. If the shell is closed, the nut hasn't yet matured.

1. Preheat oven to 350°F.
2. Beat the eggs on high speed until fluffy. Gradually add extracts and sugar until the mixture is thick and lemon colored.
3. Mix the flour with the baking powder and salt. Whisk in the egg mixture until thoroughly combined. Fold in nuts.
4. Grease a 10" × 14" strip down the center of each of two cookie sheets. Spoon half the mixture down the center of each in a 3" × 10" strip; bake for 30 minutes. Remove the baked "logs" from oven. Keep oven hot.
5. Let logs cool for 5 minutes, then cut each log diagonally into 14 slices with a serrated knife. Place on sheet and return to oven. Bake for 5 to 7 minutes. Remove to rack and let stand. Serve with peach sauce.

Cinnamon Almond Cake

Serves 12

 Total Cost: $2.36

Calories per Serving: 303

Fat: 18.5 grams

Protein: 8.8 grams

Sodium: 38.3 mg

Carbohydrates: 28.7 grams

Cholesterol: 128.2 mg

1 cup sugar

¼ teaspoon grated lemon rind

6 egg yolks

½ pound finely ground almonds

½ teaspoon cinnamon

6 egg whites

½ cup heavy cream

¼ teaspoon granulated sugar

1 teaspoon brandy

Chopped almonds, for garnish

1. Preheat oven to 350°F. Grease two 8-inch pans.
2. Cream the sugar, rind, and yolks until light and fluffy. Stir in finely ground almonds and cinnamon.
3. Whip the egg whites until stiff. Stir a few tablespoons of whites into the almond mixture and then fold in the rest.
4. Pour into greased pans; bake for 45 minutes. Let cool briefly on the racks and remove from pans.
5. Whip the cream with the sugar and brandy. Spread between cake layers and then on top and sides. Garnish with chopped almonds.

Fresh Fruit and Meringue

 Serves 12

6 egg whites

½ cup granulated sugar

¼ teaspoon cream of tartar

2 cups chopped fresh fruit

¼ teaspoon fresh-grated lemon zest

½ pound chopped almonds

3 tablespoons honey

1. Preheat oven to 200°F.
2. Line a baking sheet with parchment paper or spray with cooking spray.
3. In a copper or stainless steel bowl, beat the egg whites, sugar, and cream of tartar until stiff. Use the back of a metal spoon to spread the meringue into discs on the baking sheet. Bake in oven for 5 to 6 hours, until dry, crispy, and lightly golden. Cool meringue on the baking sheet with the oven turned off.
4. Top with fresh seasonal fruit, lemon zest, almonds, and honey.

Minted Middle Eastern Buttermilk Shake

Serves: 1

Total Cost: $3.97

Calories per Serving: 99

Fat: 2.1 grams

Protein: 8.2 grams

Sodium: 257.3 mg

Carbohydrates: 11.8 grams

Cholesterol: 9.7 mg

4 or 5 ice cubes

1 cup nonfat buttermilk

Pinch of salt

3 or 4 fresh mint leaves

1. Combine all of the ingredients in a blender. Cover and blend until no chunks of ice remain. Pour into a tall mug and garnish with more mint leaves.

INDEX

the hungry Editor

Foodies Unite!

Bring your appetite and follow The Hungry Editor who really loves to eat. She'll be discussing (and drooling over) all things low-fat and full-fat, local and fresh, canned and frozen, highbrow and lowbrow. . .

When it comes to good eats, The Hungry Editor (and her tastebuds) do not discriminate!

It's a Feeding Frenzy—dig in!

Sign up for our newsletter at
www.adamsmedia.com/blog/cooking
and download our free **Top Ten Gourmet Meals for $7** recipes!